GOD SO LOVED THE WORLD . . .

A Commentary on the Bible

JOHN J. CASTELOT, S. S.

With an Introduction by Leo J. Trese

It would be a great mistake to look upon the Bible as a mere book of inspirational reading. It would be an equally great mistake to look upon the Bible as nothing more than the story of certain men and epochs, a history of modern man's beginnings.

The Bible is much more than either of these. The Bible is inspirational, yes. It is historical, yes. But the essential nature of the Bible is that it is *salvation history*. It is the divinely inspired account of God's dealings with mankind, in which God reveals Himself progressively more clearly to His creature, man.

In the fulness of time, God incarnated Himself in Jesus Christ. Yet, long before that event, God had begun to incarnate Himself in the Sacred Scriptures. In the holy writings, God, little by little, began to make Himself visible and (to the degree that God can be understood) understandable. God gradually unfolded His plan for man, and made plain man's own part in that plan. In the Bible, God established contact with man. God confronted man, and He still confronts him and says, implicitly, "This is Who I am. What, now, is your response to this unveiling of Myself?"

God So Loved the World...

God So Loved the World...

A COMMENTARY ON THE BIBLE

by John J. Castelot, S. S.
With a foreword by Rev. Leo J. Trese

FIDES PUBLISHERS, INC. ● NOTRE DAME, INDIANA

ACKNOWLEDGMENT

Some of the material in the following chapters has already appeared in another context in the author's *Meet the Bible!* (Baltimore: Helicon Press). He gratefully acknowledges the kind permission of the publishers to adapt that material to the present purpose.

FOREWORD

It would be a great mistake to look upon the Bible as a mere book of inspirational reading. It would be an equally great mistake to look upon the Bible as nothing more than the story of certain men and epochs, a history of modern man's beginnings.

The Bible is much more than either of these. The Bible is inspirational, yes. It is historical, yes. But the essential nature of the Bible is that it is *salvation history*. It is the divinely inspired account of God's dealings with mankind, in which God reveals Himself progressively more clearly to His creature, man.

In the fulness of time God incarnated Himself in Jesus Christ. Yet, long before that event, God had begun to incarnate Himself in the Sacred Scriptures. In the holy writings God, little by little, began to make Himself visible and (to the degree that God can be understood) understandable. God gradually unfolded His plan for man, and made plain man's own part in that plan. In the Bible God established contact with man. God confronted man, as He still confronts him and says, implicitly, "This is who I am. What, now, is your response to this unveiling of Myself?"

The Bible has sometimes been compared to a sacrament. It is not actually a sacrament, because a sacrament is an action in which man cooperates with God to grow in grace. The Bible is a vision rather than an action, a vision of God which feeds our faith and helps our faith to grow. Although it is not an action, the reading of the Bible must lead to action, else the vision will have been in vain.

Our confrontation with God will be more challenging and our vision of God will be sharper if we have some appreciation of the background against which God worked. God, man's creator, could advance with His revelation only as far and as fast as man's limitations would permit. Salvation history becomes much more understandable to us when we know something of the times, the customs, the circumstances of the sacred writers and of the patriarchs and prophets and kings who people the Bible's pages. With this background knowledge we can see, for example, that God would not have dared (speaking in human terms) to be born into the world in the days of Moses or of King David. There still was too much spade-work to be done.

To illuminate salvation history for us, few men are as well equipped as Father John J. Castelot of the Society of St. Sulpice. He is an eminent Biblical scholar and a professor of Sacred Scripture. In addition to his depth of learning, Father Castelot also possesses the gift of expressing himself in a lively and lucid style. It is a pleasure, always, to read what he writes.

It is a pleasure for me, also, to have the privilege of introducing this latest work of Father Castelot. I am convinced that anyone who reads this book to the end will possess, as a result, a much more vivid understanding of God's infinite wisdom and patience and mercy as He seeks to guide back to Himself His beloved creature, man. Any reader's present fund of religious knowledge will take on new life and meaning.

— Leo J. Trese

TABLE OF CONTENTS

Part I

THE OLD TESTAMENT

THE CALL OF ABRAHAM

"The book of the origin of Jesus Christ, the Son of David, the Son of Abraham." These opening words of the Gospel of Matthew tell in capsule form the marvelous story of man's salvation. They are a joyous proclamation to the world that Jesus of Nazareth was in all truth the Christ, the Messiah sent by God to reconcile His estranged children to Himself and to lead them back to the home — so long empty — which He had prepared for them. Jesus was the glorious son of David, the ideal descendant of that ideal king, for whose coming the Jews, encouraged by their prophets, had so ardently yearned throughout the long centuries. Jesus was also the son of Abraham, that divinely chosen father of the Chosen People, the man with whom salvation history began. But why should there have been such a history at all? Because "God is love" (1 John 4:8).

At the dawn of time the Creator had lavished His love and special care on the formation of a man and a woman. Unlike the rest of earth's creatures, each of which reflected His perfections in its own pale way, these two were made to His own image and likeness. Images of Himself, a Pure Spirit, they were endowed with a spiritual nature: they were intelligent, free, and immortal. But images admit of different degrees of likeness, and so the divine Artist completed His masterpiece by conferring on these two images of Himself His very own likeness: He gave them a share in His inner life. They were not only His images; they were His friends, His children. They could know Him in the same way, though not to the same degree, as He knew Himself. They could love Him with His very own love. They were, in short, in the state of grace, that wonderful state of intimacy with the only Father either of them had ever known. The sacred author of Genesis describes this state most touchingly when he pictures God as walking in their garden in the cool of the evening, the time of day when work is done and families gather to relax and chat and find comfort in the wonder of their mutual love.

But when God came looking for His children this particular evening, He could not find them. They were hiding from Him, and it was no game they were playing. They were deadly serious, and He knew it. For He knew full well that the bond which joined them to Him had been snapped, shattered by the one force that could possibly sunder it: sin. Out of respect for their freedom, He had made their friendship with Him a matter of their choice. He had given them a command which they could keep or break. Egged on by a wily, diabolically intelligent foe, they had chosen to break it. Their choice had been free, dispassionate, deliberate. The Tempter could only suggest, he could not force, and he was well aware of the fact. So he merely suggested and hoped for the worst, and the worst happened. God's children turned their backs on Him, and His light ceased to reflect in their souls. They continued to be His images, for they still possessed their spiritual nature, but His likeness faded from their souls. Horribly defaced images, they tried to hide their ugliness from His eyes. Already they had forgotten that He sees everything.

In His justice He had to punish them. No longer were they His children; the garden which had been a bit of heaven on earth was closed to them. Gone were the delights of that garden: freedom from sickness, pain, and death. Now they must suffer and die and toil laboriously to stave off death from day to day. The warm human sentiments which had glowed pleasantly in their innocent breasts now became raging fires burning fiercely out of control. The wills which should have governed them had been weakened by their own misuse of them. And their minds, once so clear and bright, now groped in the frightening darkness of ignorance. Horribly defaced images, they could produce only such images, and thus the human family started its dismal trek across the face of the earth.

God, however, is merciful as well as just. In almost the same breath in which He announced the bitter conflict that men would have to wage with the forces of evil, He promised that one day they would be victorious. The promise was rather vague, but it was a ray of hope piercing the enveloping darkness, however feebly. Just to know that someday someone would crush the head of the archenemy was enough to inspire a glimmer of hope. This tiny spark surely must have sputtered and gone out over the long millenia, but it was not to die. One day it would revive and burst into brilliant flame.

Who can tell how many thousands of years passed before the spark began to glow again? One hundred? Five hundred? What a long time for man to endure the awful silence of God! But time and eternity are two quite different realms, and God dwells in the realm of eternity. "One day with the Lord is as a thousand years, and a thousand years as one day" (2 Pet. 3:8). At any rate, there came a day when the spark was rekindled, when the silence was broken. It was about the year 1850 B.C., and the man in whose soul the voice sounded was a Semite named Abram.

For some time he had been camping near the town of Ur, on the banks of the lower Euphrates. One of a large group of semi-nomadic people who had made their way up from the Arabian peninsula, he and his family lived in black goatskin tents. They wandered at will, settled at will, much like our own trailer population. Their flocks furnished food and clothing, and from time to time they would stop in one place long enough to raise some simple crops. Camping near a large city gave them opportunities for barter with the inhabitants, but it also brought them into contact with the seductions of a more sophisticated way of life. Ur, like so many Mesopotamian cities, was a center of polytheistic worship, and the Bible makes no secret of the fact that Abram's family were polytheists. (See Jos. 24:2.)

· Archeologists have furnished us with ample evidence that this period of history was marked by frequent mass migrations throughout the Mideast, and specifically from southern to northern Mesopotamia. Caught up in this restless movement, Thare, Abram's father, led his clan from Ur to Haran. It is rather

significant that the two cities were bound together by community
of worship, with the moon-god Sin as their chief deity. But at
Haran Abram was destined not to resume relations with the
familiar gods of Ur, but instead to enter into a unique relationship with the one true God.

In some mysterious way God illumined Abram's soul, revealed
Himself to him as the one true God, and asked him to do His
bidding. The sacred text puts the divine message in this way:

Leave your country, your kinsfolk and your father's house,
    for the land which I will show you;
    I will make a great nation of you.
I will bless you, and make your name great,
    so that you shall be a blessing.
I will bless them that bless you,
    and curse them that curse you.
In you shall all the nations of the earth be blessed (Gen. 12:1-3).

The spark had been rekindled; the promise made to "the seed
of the woman" was now repeated, but this time to a definite
individual within the framework of history. We have the advantage of hindsight and know how all the nations of the earth
have been blessed in Abram. A descendant of his has crushed
the head of the Serpent. But Abram had no such advantage.
How could he know he was not dreaming? How should he
react to this strange notion of one only God, he who had never
known anything but a multiplicity of gods? Did this intensely
personal experience of his warrant his pulling up stakes and
leaving family, friends, familiar terrain? We must assume that
the God who called him gave him the grace to respond to his
vocation, and it is to his eternal credit that he accepted the grace
and answered the call. He was pre-eminently a man of faith,
as his whole history shows, and in the strength of his faith he
walked into the unknown.

Apparently his father had died (Gen. 11:32 tells us that he
died in Haran), and so with his wife Sarai and the family of
his nephew Lot he set out for Chanaan. Upon his arrival he

was assured by God that this was the land He had promised to give to him and his descendants. Moving at a leisurely pace through the central hill-country, he came finally to the Negeb, which is now an arid wasteland but at that time was rather densely populated. While he was there a famine struck and he found it impossible to sustain his household and the livestock which had been steadily increasing. Following time-honored custom, he headed for Egypt, the breadbasket of the area. There he would be allowed to graze his herds and barter for staples, but he would be a foreigner nonetheless, unprotected by the laws of the country. Foreseeing that he would be at the mercy of local officials, he instructed Sarai to pose as his sister. The scouts of the pharao, ever on the lookout for new recruits for the royal harem, might notice her and take her to the palace. If they believed her to be his sister, they would simply take her, without further ado. But if they knew her to be his wife, they might well feel obliged to make her a widow first. Abram's fears were realized, but disaster struck the court as a result and Sarai was returned to him unharmed, along with rich gifts and an earnest plea to leave the country. This story was a favorite in the family and has come down to us in three different versions, in one of which the chief actors are Isaac and Rebecca, and in a different locale. There is no reason to doubt that it had some basis in fact, but its chief value lies in its aptness as an illustration of God's providential care of his chosen ones.

Back in Chanaan, he and Lot remained in the Negeb for a while and then made their way back north to the hill-country. By this time their flocks and herds had grown to such proportions that they made a rather unwieldy caravan. Watering places were few and far between and inevitable disputes broke out between Abram's men and those of Lot over use of them. Abram suggested that they split up amicably and, with characteristic generosity, gave Lot first choice as to where he would settle. He chose the lush Jordan valley and eventually settled in Sodom. Shortly thereafter a coalition of five kings attacked Sodom and Lot was captured. When word of this reached Abram he unhesitatingly mustered a little army of his hired hands and went in pursuit. By a series of hit-and-run guerilla attacks he succeeded in wearing down the fleeing enemy and rescued his nephew.

An interesting little episode intrudes itself into this narrative. The king of Salem (Jerusalem), Melchisedec, came out to meet Abram, apparently to conclude some sort of treaty with him, for he supplied bread and wine for a covenant meal, a sign of agreement between the contracting parties. As was the custom in those days, he was also the high priest of his city, which worshiped a deity known as El Elyon (God Most High). In this capacity he called down blessings on Abram. It is most unlikely that he was a monotheist or that he worshiped the one true God. As priest-king of a Chanaanite town, he would have shared the religious convictions of his time and place. Abram's faith was the result of a unique divine intervention! Later writers found Melchisedec an intriguing figure and used him as a type of the Messiah. Thus we read in the clearly messianic psalm 109: "Thou art a priest forever, according to the order of Melchisedec." The point of this analogy is simply that the Messiah, like Melchisedec, will combine in his person the dual dignity of king and priest. There is a further development of this typology in the Epistle to the Hebrews. But we must remember that we are dealing with analogy and resist the temptation to read back into the type all the perfections of the antitype.

But to return to Abram and Lot: when they arrived back in Sodom, Abram offered to hand over to the king of that city all the booty which he had recovered. Each new event in his life brings him more sharply into focus as a true nobleman: generous, obliging, unselfish, willing to put himself out for others.

But the grand promise of a numerous progeny was still unfulfilled, and he and Sarai were now beyond the age of parenthood. Still, God had promised, and Abram was a man of deep faith. As St. Paul was to say, he hoped against hope. To keep his hope from flagging, God repeated the promise and entered mystically into a solemn covenant with him. Sarai, however, was impatient, and in accord with the customs of the day, suggested that he take her handmaid Agar and have a child by her. When Agar conceived she began to treat Sarai with ill-disguised contempt. Infuriated, Sarai turned on poor Abram and blamed him for what was happening. With the calm dignity we should have expected of him, he replied quite simply: "Your maid is in your power; do to her what seems good to you." His wife did just that; she put Agar back in her place and quite evidently made life miserable for her. The distraught girl tried to run away, but the Lord directed her to return. She did so and in due time bore Abram a son whom she called Ismael. Once more God repeated His promise to Abram and on this occasion changed his name to Abraham — an indication of their special relationship. And he instructed him to see to it that all his male descendants should be circumcised. This would serve as a sign that they belonged to the people of promise, the Chosen People.

Eventually God did keep His promise and Sara (He had changed her name, too) bore a son whom they called Isaac. Hardly had he grown into sturdy boyhood when Abraham's faith was put to the severest test of all. God commanded him to take this lad, so long awaited, the apple of his eye, his hope for the future, and offer him in sacrifice on a distant hill. (Abraham would have seen nothing terribly unusual about the command itself, as human sacrifice was common enough at the time and he was not yet familiar with the high moral code which God was gradually to reveal.) In a narrative remarkable for its poignant restraint, the sacred author tells us of Abraham's unquestioning compliance with the Lord's request. As it turned out, God was merely testing his loyal servant's faith; and he passed the test admirably. His hand was actually raised to plunge a knife into the quivering flesh of his wide-eyed son when God stepped in and stopped him. It would be impossible to find in all of human history a more impressive example of faithful obedience to the will of God. No wonder St. Paul could look upon Abraham as the father of all the faithful, the model of all those whom God calls to believe and trust in Him.

After Sara's death, Abraham sent his steward north to find a wife for Isaac among his own blood relatives. And then, having fulfilled most remarkably his role in the drama of salvation, he died and was laid to rest alongside his wife. He died happy in the knowledge that the God who had made such glowing and seemingly fantastic promises to him had not disappointed him. The proof of it all stood there by his deathbed: Isaac, the son of promise in a double sense. He represented the fulfillment of a promise and was himself a promise of still greater fulfillment. For he would continue the line which would culminate one day in Him for whose coming God was now definitely preparing: the Son whom He would not spare but would sacrifice on a distant hilltop for man's salvation. The spark was beginning to glow, fanned by the breath of divine love.

II

THE PATRIARCHS IN EGYPT

Isaac, for all his importance as a vital link in the process of salvation history, does not stand out as a strong personality. We think of him as Abraham's son and Jacob's father; before these two key figures he pales into insignificance. Even his marriage with Rebecca is part of the Abraham story. It was he who sent his steward into upper Mesopotamia to find a suitable bride for his son, and in this venture, surely one of the most charming stories in the Bible, Isaac plays a very minor role. He simply accepts Rebecca when Eliezer brings her back; but he does receive her warmly and loves her dearly. Then she, too, forces him into the background, for generosity and warmth are not her only traits of character. She is also a girl who knows what she wants and knows how to get it.

Of the twins who were born to them, Esau made his appearance first and thus enjoyed the rights of the eldest son. His brother was literally at his heels: the sacred text tells us that he was born with his fist clutching Esau's heel. This explains the name he was given: Jacob "he follows, overtakes," from the Hebrew word for heel *('aqeb)*. Subsequent events were to bear out the aptness of his name.

The story of the two brothers is a fascinating study of two types of men: the rugged man of action and the thinker. Esau grew up to be what would be known in some circles today as "a real boy," and he was Isaac's pride and joy. Robust, self-reliant, he would spend weeks at a time out in the desert, camping and hunting. But he was also rather stupid and learned too late that sheer brawn and animal cunning were no match for calculated shrewdness.

It was his brother who taught him this lesson, and it was a costly one. Jacob was the exact opposite. Not that he was a physical weakling — there is ample evidence to the contrary — but he was a homebody. One rather suspects that he was tied to Rebecca's apron strings. He was definitely her favorite, and she meant to see that he got all that was coming to him; more, if possible. One day Esau staggered home after an unsuccessful hunting expedition. Exhausted and famished, he would have given his right arm for a square meal. And there was Jacob cooking, of all things, and scheming, too. Esau begged for some food and his brother, quickly sizing up the situation, decided that this was his chance. He proposed a hard bargain: some food in exchange for Esau's birthright. At the moment Esau couldn't have cared less about his position as firstborn; he was hungry and solemnly agreed to the bargain. The sacred writer is plainly aghast at his animality: "He ate and drank and went his way. Thus lightly did Esau value his birthright" (Gen. 25:34). It was an undeniably shady transaction, but it was perfectly legal. Jacob had played his first card, but by no means his last.

About this time there occurred at Bersabee an incident which illustrates most graphically what was said above about Isaac's taking a back seat to his great father Abraham — not to mention his wife Rebecca and his son Jacob. "The LORD appeared to him that very night and said, 'I am the God of your father Abraham; fear not, for I am with you. I will bless you and multiply your descendants for the sake of my servant Abraham' " (Gen. 26:23-24). "For the sake of my servant Abraham!" Later, when Esau married two (!) Hittite girls, it was only at Rebecca's nagging insistence that Isaac ordered Jacob to choose a wife from his own clan. Poor Isaac! Even his deathbed was lumpy.

Sensing that his end was near, he asked Esau to go out and kill some game so that he could enjoy one last favorite meal. Little did he know that Rebecca had her ear to the partition of the tent and was cooking up not a last meal but a scheme that would clinch Jacob's position in the family. Isaac had told Esau that when he served him the desired meal he would give him his last blessing, a blessing of profound significance among the Semites. Determined that Jacob and not Esau should benefit by it, she masterminded a plot to further this purpose. She would prepare a dish to taste just like Esau's hunter's stew and Jacob, dressed in his brother's clothes and with goat hairs on his hands and neck to simulate Esau's hairiness, would serve it to the dying man and obtain his blessing. The poor old man's eyes weren't what they used to be, and he would have to rely on his sense of touch and smell.

The ruse worked, even though Isaac was a bit suspicious at first, and Jacob received the treasured blessing, which was considered irrevocable even if obtained under false pretenses. It is difficult not to feel sorry for the poor hulking Esau when he learns how he has been outwitted and tearfully begs for just a little blessing. Brains had triumphed over brawn again, but it was not a pretty sight. Jacob's action was downright despicable, and the fact that he was following his mother's importunate orders is no excuse. After all, he was a grown man, and his apprehension at her mention of the scheme shows that he knew he was doing something very wrong.

How, then, did he merit to be the father of the twelve tribes who would play such an important role in God's plan for man's salvation? The fact is that he merited nothing; nor did his father or his father's father before him. It was God who, out of sheer loving-kindness, took the initiative in calling Abraham, in protecting and guiding his descendants. He took them as they were, turning even their faults to good account, leading them step by step, generation by generation, to ever fuller knowledge of the truth, ever more noble conduct. As a people, they had a long, long way to go, and many a backward step they took in the process. God chose to work out man's salvation within the framework of human history, and human history is not all sweetness and light. From time to time He would act in a special way on the soul of an individual, as He did in the case of Abraham and as He was one day to do in the case of Jacob. But ordinarily He took His instruments just as they were, patiently leading them onward, like a skilled teacher who knows he will not produce geniuses or saints overnight. Who knew human nature better than its Creator? Who respected human freedom more than He who had entrusted the destiny of the race to the free will of its progenitors? No, the patriarchs were not saints. How far they were from that ideal will become increasingly and often shockingly clear. And it is to the eternal credit of the sacred historians that they glossed over none of the glaring defects of their revered ancestors.

His status at home well secured, Jacob went north to visit his uncle Laban and to find a wife from among his cousins. He fell in love with Rachel and agreed to an adoption-marriage contract with her father. Laban at that time had no son and was glad to have a man around the house to look after his affairs. He legally adopted Jacob, granting him rights which would have been enjoyed by a natural son had he had one. In return for Rachel's hand, Jacob agreed to work for him for seven years. But Jacob the schemer had met his match. On the wedding night Laban substituted another daughter, Lia, whose prospects apparently were not too bright, and by the time Jacob discovered the fraud he had taken her to wife. So great was his love for Rachel, however, that he agreed to an additional seven years' service. She and Lia and two concubines, Bala and Zelpha, bore him twelve sons and a daughter. The sons, future fathers of the twelve tribes of Israel, were called: Ruben, Simeon, Levi, Juda, Issachar, Zabulon (born of Lia); Joseph and Benjamin (born of Rachel); Dan and Nephtali (born of Bala); Gad and Aser (born of Zelpha). The daughter's name was Dina.

Jacob's stay with Laban was a long battle of wits with his shrewd uncle. In the end Jacob came out on top and headed home with his large family, flocks, and possessions. Over the years he had matured considerably. Away from Rebecca and with a family of his own to care for, he had developed real strength of character. Not that he had undergone a complete personality change; he was still as calculating and as shrewd as ever, but he had improved noticeably. And on the way back to Chanaan he had an intense religious experience, an encounter with God which capped the maturing process. This vision is described — to the extent that such an experience can be described — in Gen. 32:25-33. In the course of it his name was changed to Israel, just as Abram's had been changed to Abraham. Accordingly, his descendants were known henceforth as "sons of Israel" or Israelites.

At the moment the Israelites were a family. They would one day become a nation, but the birth of that nation, like all births, was to be accompanied by much pain and travail. The sons of Jacob were, by and large, a rough lot, at times ruthless, savage — even fratricidal. Witness their reckless sack of Sichem, Ruben's incest with his father's concubine, Juda's dalliance with his daughter-in-law Thamar in the guise of a temple prostitute, the apparent nonchalance of their decision to kill Joseph for the simple reason that he got on their nerves.

Joseph, son of Rachel, who had died giving birth to Benjamin, was clearly his father's pet, and Jacob most unwisely doted on him. The boy was a dreamer, and his dreams were dreams of grandeur in which he saw himself lording it over his brothers. With boyish ingenuousness he chattered about these dreams until even Jacob got a bit piqued. The brothers were more than just piqued; they were annoyed and angry. One day, when they were grazing their flocks at some distance from home, Jacob sent Joseph to see how they were doing. When they saw him coming, they decided — with appalling cold-blood — to kill him. But Ruben — or Juda, according to another tradition — dissuaded them. They compromised by selling him to an Egypt-bound caravan as a slave. His precious cloak, a special gift from Jacob, they smeared with goat's blood and sent back to Jacob, who could only conclude that the boy had been killed by a wild animal.

In Chanaan, Joseph's dreams had been his downfall. In Egypt dreams were to serve him well. He was sold as a household slave to a government official and immediately proceeded to ingratiate himself with his master, who soon appreciated his fine qualities and reposed great confidence in him. Unfortunately, the official's wife also found him most attractive — indeed, irresistible — and attempted to seduce him. He staunchly refused, and his indignant reply indicates a belief — unique in those times — in a God who took a dim view of such proceedings: "How then can I commit this great crime, and sin against God?" (Gen. 39:9). Stung by the rebuff, the wife raised a great hue and cry and accused Joseph of attacking her. The outraged husband threw him into prison.

Here, too, Joseph's charm and manifest administrative skill — or rather the extraordinary Providence so evident throughout his whole career — saw him through. The warden gave him charge of all the other prisoners, who were mostly of the political variety. Among them were the pharao's chief butler and baker. Each of them had a dream which Joseph correctly interpreted as pointing to the butler's release and the baker's execution. The butler was understandably delighted and grateful, but when he was set free and reinstated three days later, he promptly proceeded to forget all about Joseph. But two years later the pharao himself had a dream which stumped all the court interpreters. The butler then remembered Joseph, who explained the dream as meaning that seven years of plenty would be followed by seven years of famine in Egypt. With some of the ingenuousness of his boyhood, he suggested that a clever administrator be chosen to arrange for the conservation and distribution of grain over the next fourteen years. He was given the job on the spot.

When the famine struck Egypt was prepared for it, but Chanaan was not. Jacob was hard hit and sent his sons to Egypt to purchase grain. They were directed to Joseph, who recognized them without being recognized in turn. He so arranged matters that eventually he had the whole family with him in Egypt. Their reunion is surely one of the most touching scenes in the Old Testament. The pharao himself welcomed them and gave them a generous land grant in the fertile eastern delta region. Here they were to stay for the next few centuries. Apparently not all the Israelites came into Egypt on this occasion and it seems likely that from time to time groups of them wandered back to Chanaan. These probabilities would go a long way towards explaining some of the events in the later history of the people. But the majority of them did come and settle and stay. The Bible tells us nothing of their long sojourn. We can only surmise that for a long time they grew and prospered, some drifting into the cities to engage in commercial enterprises, intermarrying with the Egyptians, learning a great deal about civilization and culture, both of which were at that time very old in Egypt. The great pyramids, eloquent monuments to almost incredible engineering and administrative ability, had been standing for almost 500 years when Joseph welcomed his clan to their new home.

God's providential guidance of His chosen ones stands out in sharp relief in this whole affair. The Lord of history had selected just the right moment for Joseph to appear on the Egyptian scene. For at that time the country was ruled by invaders, at least largely Semitic, who had taken over the reigns of government. These usurpers, known as Hyksos, ruled from 1710 to 1570 B.C. It is quite understandable that they would be ready to acknowledge the ability of a fellow Semite and entrust to him a key position in the government. They would feel no uneasiness about installing a large group of Semites in a lush section of the country quite near the strategic northeast border. An Egyptian regime would hardly have been so sympathetic. In fact, when the Egyptians finally succeeded in ousting the Hyksos and regaining control, they proved most unsympathetic. But that, too, was part of the divine plan.

Jacob died in Egypt, was embalmed in the Egyptian manner, and was escorted back to Chanaan for burial in the land of his fathers. The cortege returned to Egypt and there Joseph and his brothers breathed their last. The Age of the Patriarchs, strictly so called, had ended, and with it the first era of salvation history. The sojourn in Egypt was a sort of interlude, a preparation of the raw material which Moses would fuse into a nation, the nation of Israel, the People of God.

III

MOSES AND THE EXODUS

Rome wasn't built in a day, and neither was Israel. When the family of Jacob went down into Egypt they would hardly have made up a good sized village, let alone a nation. It was to take many generations for the budding family to grow to national proportions. Even more important than numerical strength was that inner self-consciousness which would give them an awareness of being a distinct political, religious, and cultural entity. Our own original thirteen colonies did not become a nation overnight or without a struggle. If a people is to survive and prosper, it must possess the requisite skills: political, legal, technical, commercial, agricultural, military, and all the rest. The metamorphosis of a clan of seminomads into a strong independent nation was going to take a lot of doing.

The sojourn in Egypt, then, was positively providential, part of God's master plan. Living as foreigners in relative isolation, the Israelites were constantly and increasingly sensitive to the fact that they did not really belong, that they were "different." This group consciousness drew them closer and closer together into a distinct unit. They treasured their family traditions, and since the religious element was such an essential factor in those traditions, they preserved the unique religion of their ancestors. It would be rather naive to believe that they were completely uncontaminated by the religious beliefs and practices of the Egyptians, especially since they lacked any well-defined leadership in religious matters. But they seem to have held on to the essentials and, little by little, developed a culture all their own. Their proximity to the border of Chanaan enabled them to maintain contact with the past and to meet, at least sporadically, with relatives whose forefathers had not come down to Egypt or who had returned to Chanaan. Finally, their language set them apart rather effectively. The patriarchs had adopted Chanaanite, an older form of Hebrew, as their family language, and their descendants continued to speak it. What more natural than for people speaking the same idiom to stay pretty much to themselves?

In spite of all this, they could not help being affected by their surroundings. As Providence would have it, the time of their sojourn was one of the most brilliant periods of Egyptian history, that of the New Empire. Architecture, building, art, and literature were all flourishing vigorously at this time, and the Israelites watched, admired, and learned. Undoubtedly many of them made their way into the financial and commercial whirl of the prosperous country, and we shall soon see the part they played in the construction projects of the pharaos. This, of course, would best be classified as compulsory education, but it was an education nonetheless, and a providential one, too. For they would hand on their skills to their descendants, and they, in turn, would put them to good use one day. They could not help observing the marvelous administrative organization that kept the great nation running smoothly and efficiently. Militarily, too, Egypt was in its heyday. After the native rulers had expelled the Hyksos interlopers in the sixteenth century, they pushed north and re-established their former supremacy over Chanaan and part of Syria. The Egypt of the New Empire was, then, a splendid school in which to learn the complicated and many-sided business of becoming a strong and self-sufficient nation. Not that they were conscious of this destiny of theirs; but He who had fixed this destiny for them knew whither they were heading and was readying them.

The man selected by Providence to guide their first faltering steps in this direction was exceptionally well equipped for the task. His name was Moses — but to understand even the circumstances of his birth we must have some idea of the cruel world into which he was born. After the Egyptians had regained control of their country they became understandably sensitive to foreign elements in their midst. Even so, they seem to have left the Israelites alone for quite a while. This may have been due to the fact that they re-established the center of government in the south, far from the area in which the Hebrews lived. But Seti I (1302-1290) moved the capital back to the delta region and began an extensive rebuilding program which was carried forward most energetically by his successor, Ramses II (1290-1224). Either of these two could have been the "new king, who knew nothing of Joseph" (Ex. 1:8). They would have known nothing of the services Joseph had rendered the nation centuries before or of the fact that the Israelites were there with the full consent of the pharao of Joseph's day. Not that that would have helped much, for that particular pharao had been one of the detested Hyksos.

Ramses especially would have resented and feared their presence, for he had to keep up a running battle with menacing Asiatics all throughout his long reign. Here was a potentially powerful group of Semites parked right near his most strategic border. No wonder he addressed his subjects as follows: "Look how numerous and powerful the Israelite people are growing, more so than we ourselves! Come, let us deal shrewdly with them to stop their increase; otherwise, in time of war they too may join our enemies to fight against us, and so leave our country" (Ex. 1:9-10). He didn't want to lose them, for they were too valuable as slave labor, but he did want to weaken their military potential. To this end he instituted a program of cruel oppression. One of the measures called for the murder of all male Hebrews at birth.

A certain Hebrew woman of the tribe of Levi gave birth to a son about that time and her fear that he would be taken from her triggered an ingenious plan. She had noticed that the pharao's daughter frequently came down with her maids to bathe in the branch of the Nile which ran near her home. Gambling on the royal lady's womanly instincts, she fashioned a little basket of strips of papyrus, made it watertight, and placed it at a strategic spot near the riverbank. She also posted her daughter Miriam as a lookout. Her gamble paid off. The pharao's daughter was captivated by the chubby little baby and immediately looked about for a nursemaid. Miriam was right there and suggested her mother, who thus had the pleasure of nursing her baby and the reassurance that it would live. When the child was weaned she dutifully delivered him to the pharao's daughter, who called him Moses (from the Egyptian *mosu,* "son").

The boy grew up in the palace which his compatriots had been forced to build and received an education on a par with that of all the young men of the court. The Israelites were to need a wise leader, and Providence was preparing one for them. But for all his good fortune, the young man was not unmindful of the people from whom he had sprung. As Father Ricciotti puts it:

> While he was enjoying a life of ease at court, he could not help coming into contact with Israelites in the vicinity who were being forced to make bricks and to labor at the building of Pi-Rameses. His ears, which were habitually soothed by the skillful music of the court harpists and by the caressing voices of handmaids reading aloud their fantastic Egyptian

stories, were suddenly assaulted by the cries of pain uttered by the builders, his brothers, as they were beaten by the Egyptian inspectors. The city that arose was indeed beautiful, but to the eyes of the reflective courtier its bricks dripped blood. *(The History of Israel,* I, 174-5.)

One day he came upon a taskmaster flogging a Hebrew slave and in a blind rage slew him on the spot. This constituted treason, and he had to flee the country.

He headed east to Madian, where he married a girl named Sepphora and tended the flocks of her father Jethro. Providence again! Roaming with his flocks in search of pasturage, he gained intimate firsthand knowledge of precisely that terrain over which he would have to guide his people to safety in the not too distant future. One day, out there in the wilderness of Sinai, he had an encounter with God, a religious experience which had a profound effect on him; it set him on the path to greatness. In his vision, God, who identified Himself as the God of the patriarchs, revealed to him His sacred name: Yahweh, which means "He is." Many interpretations of this name have been proposed, but the one that best fits all the circumstances is that which sees in it an affirmation of God's active existence, His supreme ability and readiness to act in favor of His people. Certainly Moses needed this assurance; he was scared out of his wits. And his people would need it, too, for they had been slowly but surely developing that dehumanizing slave mentality, that devastating lack of initiative which reduces man to the level of a pack animal, not caring much what happens as long as he is fed and given a place to curl up and sleep at the end of the day. It was as leader of such a people that God now appointed Moses, charging him with the fantastic task of persuading the pharao to let them return to their native land. Fantastic? Yes; actually ridiculous from a human point of view. But Moses' point of view was no longer merely human. He now saw things through Yahweh's eyes and was given divine assurance that he would succeed.

Success did not come easily, but the struggle itself served to impress upon the minds of the beaten Israelites that their God was indeed all-powerful. The forces of nature, the mighty pharao, the vaunted gods of Egypt — all were impotent before Him. Moses' first request for the liberation of the people was met with a spiteful imposition of even harsher labor, a turn of events which didn't exactly raise his stock in their eyes. But a series of calamities drew broader and broader concessions from the pharao. These calamities, known as the Ten Plagues, were, except for the last, not unusual phenomena in Egypt. In fact, we are not sure of the exact number of them. Our present account is a fusion of three different traditions, each of which preserved the memory of a certain number of plagues. Joined together they give ten. In addition, these traditions were influenced by meditation and liturgical recital over the centuries as the people recalled prayerfully and wonderingly their obviously providential deliverance from servitude. But while the details may be uncertain, the basic facts are undeniable: by an extraordinary succession of events Yahweh liberated His people, under Moses' leadership, from bondage in Egypt. Many of these events may have had a natural substratum, but they were clearly providential and just as clearly under the control of Yahweh's envoy, Moses.

The tenth plague was the death of all the firstborn, and it was the occasion of the institution of the greatest of the Hebrew feasts, the Passover or Pasch. The Israelites were instructed to slay a spotless lamb and sprinkle his blood on their doorposts. This would be a sign to the angel of death to "pass over" their homes. Then they were to roast the lamb whole and eat it with a salad of bitter herbs, standing and dressed for immediate departure. The description of the feast in Exodus contains elements which reflect a later development of this simple ceremony, and the feast of Azymes or unleavened bread seems to have been originally a separate feast which was later joined to the celebration of the Passover. At any rate, this ceremony served and still serves as a perpetual reminder to the Jews of God's loving care for His people.

Our gospels witness to the fact that the early Christians saw another providential aspect of this feast, as indeed they did of the whole Exodus. Christ as the new Moses freed His people from the slavery of sin, leading them through the waters of baptism into the Promised Land of His Kingdom. He was the true Lamb of God whose blood was shed to save all men from eternal death. John the Baptist, for example, pointed Him out to his disciples as "the lamb of God, who takes away the sin of the world" (John 1:29). It was no mere coincidence that Jesus chose to institute the Eucharist within the framework of the Passover meal and to die on the great day itself. St. John the Evangelist, recording the fact that the soldiers did not break Jesus' legs, recalls one of the prescriptions regarding the paschal lamb: "Not a bone of him shall you break" (19:36). Indeed, John's whole presentation of the Christ-event is a masterfully subtle development of the Exodus theme, and this same theme plays an important part in the other gospels, too, especially that of Matthew. God was preparing His people with a very definite end in view, and all the important elements in that preparation were to find transcendent realization in the event towards which they were converging.

The tenth plague struck terror into the hearts of all the Egyptians, from the pharao on down, and the Israelites were allowed to leave. The most direct route into Chanaan would have been northeast along the Mediterranean coastal road. But this very strategic route was crawling with Egyptian military patrols, and so they turned south, in the general direction of the mountain where God was waiting to claim them for His own. Not long after their departure the pharao regretted his decision and sent a detachment of chariots to turn them back. But Yahweh, having brought them this far, was not going to abandon them. They were camped near a narrow and relatively shallow, though unfordable, strip of water joining the main body of the Reed Sea (translated Red Sea in the Greek version) with the Bitter Lakes to the north, in the region of what is now the Suez Canal. A hot desert wind blew all night and forced the water back in either direction, thus enabling them to cross in the morning. The pursuing Egyptians were halfway across when the waters flowed back with considerable force and trapped them hopelessly.

The peninsula of Sinai, where they now found themselves, is a wildly beautiful place. When we hear of the "wandering in the desert," we are inclined to visualize vast stretches of rolling, shifting, sand dunes. Sinai is not this type of desert. The soil is gritty and stony, the vegetation is scrubby and sparse, but the mountains give the area an undeniable grandeur. They are wrinkled with age, almost scowling, but the clear sunlight, streaming down from a cloudless blue sky, makes them look soft and pink. This is all well and good for the modern tourist-pilgrim, with his Kodachrome-packed camera and a more or less comfortable car to get him to Mt. Sinai and back to Cairo. It was quite another picture for the Israelites. They had to stumble along under the relentless sun, burdened down with all their belongings. The oases, sole sources of water, were few and far between. For many, the first sweet taste of freedom soon turned bitter, and they actually thought back with longing to their slave days, when at least they could count on three square meals a day and fresh water to drink.

Far from being as yet a well-knit unit, neatly organized and motivated by singleness of purpose, they were quite a mixed, and mixed up, crowd. If they had any one goal binding them all together it was a negative one: to get away from Egypt. The mass of them were Israelites, but malcontents of all sorts must have profited by the confusion to escape with them. And along the way, groups of nomads from the peninsula quite probably fell in with the giant parade.

Here in this forbidding wasteland the straggling, grumbling, mob was to be whipped into shape as a nation, a people: God's People. The most telling factors in this process were the events which took place at Mt. Sinai, where God formally adopted them as His own, imposed obligations on them, entered into an intimate alliance with them. This alliance became the charter of all future relations between God and man. It was given perfect expression and eternal sanction in the New Covenant, sealed in the blood of the Lamb of God on another mountain: Calvary.

IV

MOSES AND THE COVENANT

"I will be your God, and you shall be my people." This, quite simply, was the agreement, the pact, the covenant, which Yahweh was to seal with the Israelites at Mt. Sinai. An amazing thing, that God should choose a nation to be His very own, and especially one which had so little to recommend it! As a later author was to remark: "It was not because you are the largest of all nations that the LORD set his heart on you and chose you, for you are really the smallest of all nations. It was because the LORD loved you and because of his fidelity to the oath he had sworn to your fathers ..." (Deut. 7:7-8). Indeed, Israel was not a nation at all; it had no unity, no homogeneity, no administrative organization, not even a land to call its own. But it did have the divine promise, made once to Abraham and often repeated, and now apparently on its way to fulfillment.

The wonders of the liberation from Egypt and the crossing of the Red Sea were calculated to strengthen the faith of the people in that promise, to inspire the confidence and initiative necessary to overcome the lethargy induced by years of hopeless servitude. God was preparing His people in advance for the relationship He would establish with them, giving them heartening assurance of His love and paternal care. They needed such assurance, and He knew it. With typical slave mentality, they complained bitterly of life in the desert: "Would that we had died at the LORD's hand in the land of Egypt, as we sat by our fleshpots and ate our fill of bread! But you had to lead us into the desert to make the whole community die of famine"

(Ex. 16:3). They wanted freedom, but not at any price. Better to be well-fed animals than hungry freemen. But God knew what they had been through, and with the patience of a loving father for a pack of whimpering children, He fed them in a striking manner.

Again He made use of a natural phenomenon to produce a result surpassing the natural. There is in the peninsula of Sinai a type of insect which feeds greedily on the tamarisk trees of the region. These insects are low on carbohydrates but have little need for sugar. So they absorb the former and exude the latter in tiny gum drops which fall to the ground and harden into edible little pellets during the cool of night. This substance is still the only source of sugar available to the Bedouin of Sinai, and they still call it manna. However, it is available for only a few months of the year and the total yield would hardly exceed a few hundred pounds. The Israelites apparently had it year round in sufficient quantities to satisfy them all. And the unusual qualities ascribed to it in Ex. 16 clearly mark it off as quite unusual. Centuries later Jesus was to use this "manna from heaven" as a type of the real heavenly food with which He was to feed His children (see John 6).

Little by little the people's respect for Yahweh's power, their confidence in the reality of His concern for them, was growing. And a rudimentary administration was set up at the suggestion of Moses' father-in-law, Jethro, who came out to meet him. How true to life that he should immediately start telling his son-in-law how to run things! But his suggestion was a good one. Moses had been trying to do everything himself: lead the march, pick the camp sites, settle the interminable squabbles that broke out — and it was simply impossible. Jethro pointed out this impossibility and suggested that he divide the people into groups and make some of the more outstanding men responsible for the conduct of the individual groups. Thus, by the time they reached Mt. Sinai they were in fairly good temper and had an organization which assured at least some measure of orderliness.

The peninsula of Sinai is shaped like a triangle. It is about 250 miles long and about 150 miles wide at its base. Near its southern tip, which is mountainous, is Mt. Sinai, called also Horeb in the Bible. Here Moses had encountered Yahweh; here Yahweh was waiting to make the Israelites His own and to start them on the way to true nationhood. Their meeting with Him was a profound religious experience, one that really defied description. Subsequent generations meditated on this transforming encounter and recounted it in their religious assemblies, expressing it in the conventional terms which were accepted ways of describing divine interventions: fire, smoke, thunder, lightning, etc. Eventually this stylized interpretation of the great event was committed to writing under divine inspiration. We must not expect of it the detailed accuracy of a newsreel; but that is not to imply that it does not record a real historical occurrence. Indeed, apart from Sinai the whole subsequent history of Israel is simply inexplicable, unintelligible. The experience of the people there bordered on the mystical, and the mystical rarely lends itself to any description other than the symbolic.

The Covenant of Sinai was a pact between Yahweh and Israel by which He adopted them as His own special possession and imposed corresponding obligations on them. It is described in terms of a type of treaty which was in vogue at that time, the suzerainty treaty. The purpose of this type of treaty was to assure the loyalty and obedience of the king's vassals. The preamble contained the king's name and extolled his greatness. This was followed by a record of the past relations between the two parties, with stress on the king's kindness and concern. Then the king imposed the required obligations on the vassals, high on the list of which was the prohibition against dealings with alien powers. The document was usually kept in the temple and read during the great feasts, when large crowds gathered. The parallels between this type of treaty, which was in vogue between 1450 and 1200 B.C., and the Covenant of Sinai are striking. See, for example, Ex. 20:1-2 and Jos. 24:2-13; Ex.

20:3, 22 and Jos. 24:14-16; Ex. 25:16. That the Israelites should have chosen this means of expressing their covenant relationship with Yahweh is a reflection of their view of that covenant. Yahweh was their King, they His vassals. He had chosen them; His choice called for a response on their part, a response involving acceptance of His will.

The divine will found expression in the Decalogue and the Code of the Alliance. The word Decalogue comes from two Greek words meaning ten and words; we know it more familiarly as the Ten Commandments. In the form in which the latter appear in Ex. 20:1-17, some of them are considerably expanded. Originally they were very probably quite short and direct, as they are in the catechism. Short or long, they express the fundamental, essential, requirements of the covenant relationship. All subsequent legislation was but a development and application of these requirements, which very clearly express the basically religious character of Israelite law.

An example of this legislation follows in the Code of the Alliance or Book of the Covenant (Ex. 20:22 — 23:19). This code contains (1) rules governing worship; (2) civil and penal laws; (3) laws covering social morality. Although it gives evidence of some later development, it undoubtedly contains much ancient material, some of it going back directly to Moses. For example, in the regulations for worship, the possibility of a number of altars in different places is clearly envisioned. Later, during the Deuteronomic reform which took place during the reign of Josias (about 621 B.C.), the principle of unity of sanctuary was rigidly enforced, limiting the worship of Yahweh to the temple at Jerusalem. On the other hand, we must not be so naive as to imagine that Yahweh presented the Law to Moses in a morocco-bound first edition or on a delicately inscribed parchment scroll. With God's approval and sanction, the great legislator of the Hebrews drew up a corpus of law on the model of existing legal codes and infused it with the spirit of the true religion. In this connection, it is interesting to compare the Mosaic Code with the Code of Hammurabi:

CH	Exodus
250. If an ox going along the street injures and kills a man, this case has no claim.	**21:28** When an ox gores a man or a woman to death, the ox must be stoned; its flesh may not be eaten. The owner of the ox, however, shall go unpunished.
251. If anyone's ox is given to goring and has shown that goring is his vice, but he (the owner) did not cut his horns or confine him; if this ox wounds and kills the son of a freeman, let him give one half mina of silver.	**29** But if an ox was previously in the habit of goring people and its owner, though warned, would not keep it in; should it then kill a man or a woman, not only must the ox be stoned, but its owner also must be put to death.
	30 If, however, a fine is imposed on him, he must pay in ransom for his life whatever amount is imposed on him.
196. If anyone has struck out the eye of the son of a freeman, his eye shall be struck out.	**21:23** But if injury ensues, you shall give life for life,
197. If he has broken the bone of a freeman, his bone shall be broken.	**24** eye for eye, tooth for tooth, hand for hand, foot for foot,
200. If anyone has knocked out the tooth of an equal to himself, his tooth shall be knocked out.	**25** burn for burn, wound for wound, stripe for stripe.

Incidentally, the principle laid down in these last verses, the so-called Lex Talionis or Law of Strict Retaliation, crude as it may seem to us, was actually a great step forward in the development of civilized law. Formerly, retribution for wrongs had been demanded with no sense of proportion at all, and this had led to endless bloody feuds. In the early part of Genesis, when the sacred author is illustrating the degrading effects of the first sin, he adduces the example of Lamech, who was a bigamist and an all-round savage. Here is his boast:

"Ada and Sella, hear my voice,
       wives of Lamech, give ear to my speech:

> I kill a man for wounding me,
>   a youth for bruising me.
> If Cain shall be avenged sevenfold,
>   Lamech seventy times sevenfold" (Gen. 4:23-24).

One day divine Justice and Mercy incarnate was to answer Peter's question, "Lord, how often shall my brother sin against me, and I forgive him? Up to seven times?" with the words, "I do not say to thee seven times, but seventy times seven" (Matt. 18:21-22). He was also to perfect the Law of Retaliation by urging that justice be tempered by the most delicate charity, but that law, when first promulgated, was still a giant step forward. It established at least some equitable proportion between crime and punishment.

From a technically juridical point of view, the Mosaic Law was in many ways inferior to other ancient legal codes, but in its ethical and religious aspects it was vastly superior to them. It regulated not only the ordinary life of the people, but was also the basis of ethics and cult. It stood as a "revelation" from God, for it was promulgated by Moses and his disciples in His name and with this noble goal: to form a priestly kingdom and a holy people (Ex. 19:6). Even if Moses adopted ancient usages, he also adapted them, redirected them to Yahweh. Whatever he borrowed from the common fund of ancient oriental legal usage he infused with the spirit of the true religion.

The Law embraced the whole man and extended to all circumstances of life, with a notable stress on interior dispositions or intentions. Many of its prescriptions may strike us as strange, especially the cleanliness and dietary laws. We are apt to wonder why a sacred law should be so minutely concerned with matters which are more hygienic than moral; some of the topics it treats are rather embarrassingly physical. But our point of view is so different from that of the ancients. We have grown up in a national tradition which is very sensitive to relationships between Church and state. We have what amounts to a fetish for specialization, departmentalization, and it is reflected in the lamentable divorce of religion from life so common in our culture. There are so many Sunday-morning Christians among us. For the Hebrews, on the other hand, religion was life. They were not just a nation; they were God's own people. He was their king who had entered into a unique covenant with them and was consequently interested in everything they did. What they did set them apart from all other nations of the earth, made them different, and kept them aware of their distinctiveness. Other peoples could do this, that, and the other thing, eat whatever they wanted, indulge their various appetites as they pleased; they could not. For they belonged to a holy God, a transcendent God, the absolute Norm of morality and holiness, and they had been called to be holy precisely because He was holy. This awareness of being different had to be kept alive to prevent compromise with the pagan principles and practices of their neighbors. The Law fulfilled this vital function.

The Israelites left Sinai to start the arduous march to nationhood. It would be a long and difficult journey, but now at least they knew where they were going. The incident of the Golden Calf is a dramatic indication that they had not been changed overnight into a nation of saints, but at least they now had a divinely sanctioned and definite blueprint for sanctity. The events of the exodus had drawn them together in confident hope for the future. Yahweh had demonstrated over and over again His love and His power as well as His transcendent and demanding holiness. He had a plan for them, a sublime destiny in human history. It was up to them now, with His help, to fulfill that plan, to realize that destiny. They were the agents of the covenant and would prepare for the eventual establishment of the new and eternal covenant, the supreme expression of God's love for mankind.

V

THE PROMISED LAND

One thought was now uppermost in the minds of all: to take possession of the land promised to the patriarchs, to become in all truth a nation, with mountains and valleys and pastures and homes to call their own. The year spent in the shadow of Mt. Sinai had been profitable in many ways. Among other things, they had got to know each other better, had developed a more definite inner organization, had become familiar with their own liturgy as celebrated at their portable temple, the Tabernacle. Here, in the Holy of Holies, was kept the Ark of the Covenant, a gold-plated chest *(arca* in Latin) containing the stone tablets on which were inscribed the Ten Commandments, the heart of the covenant. Next to this inner sanctum was an area twice as long but just as wide (30′ x 15′); here were the altar of incense, the table on which were kept twelve fresh loaves representing the constant presence of the 12 tribes before Yahweh, and the seven-branched candlestick. Finally, in a large unroofed area were the altar of sacrifice and the laver, a large basin for ritual purifications. This rather involved complex of tents and curtains and hangings was the center of their whole existence. Yahweh was conceived as dwelling over the two cherubim atop the Ark. Or rather, since the Israelites knew full well that He could not be contained in any such space, the Ark was the symbol of His active, beneficent presence among them.

At last the day came when the Tabernacle was dismantled and folded and the journey to Chanaan began. Events soon proved that the year at Sinai had not sufficed to transform the paralyzing slave mentality of the Israelites into the conquering spirit which they would need for the challenging venture which lay ahead. Whining, complaining, and near-mutiny marked their path. Nor is this hard to understand. The peninsula of Sinai is a most inhospitable region. The sun knows no mercy, and temperatures of 120 are not unusual. Water is scarce, fruit practically nonexistent. Bodily discomfort alone would have given tempers a raw edge, and in such a large crowd there were inevitably many congenital troublemakers ready to foment discontent.

One source of restlessness was the unvarying uniformity of the diet. Marvelous though the manna was, it was not overly palatable, and the people were getting sick and tired of it. Little by little the grumbling increased in volume and Moses, ever mindful of the fact that the manna had been provided by Yahweh and stood between them all and starvation, threw up his hands in disgust. He cried to the Lord for help in dealing with this self-centered, ungrateful mob. The Lord reassured him and instructed him to divide his cares among 70 reliable elders. At least he wouldn't have to listen to *all* the complaints. Yahweh went even further. The people had turned up their noses at His food and had yearned for meat such as they had eaten in Egypt. All right, He would send them meat, but it would prove their undoing. Just about this time of the year, huge flocks of quail pass over Sinai on their migration from Europe to Africa. After their nonstop flight over the Mediterranean they are weak and tired, and when they land to rest they are easily caught. Such a migration took place at this time and the people, with almost delirious greed, stuffed themselves with the rare flesh. Their fare was fowl, and it turned out to be foul fare. An epidemic of food poisoning broke out among them, and the uncounted dead were buried where they fell.

This was just one in a series of rebellions, but in each of them Yahweh vindicated His own wisdom and the authority of Moses. One of the most serious involved the very brother and sister of Moses, Aaron and Miriam. In another, a man named Core instigated a revolt against Moses and Aaron on the grounds that there was no need for an official priesthood, since all the Israelites had been called by God to be a priestly kingdom, a holy nation. Their rallying-cry has had many echoes in the course of history, but Yahweh answered it in unmistakably clear fashion.

Still another was the rebellion of Dathan and Abiram, and again God supported His chosen representative.

These few examples will suffice to indicate that the road from slavery to nationhood, from Egypt to Chanaan, was a rocky one indeed. But the goal was coming nearer and nearer. When they had reached a point just south of the Negeb they sent a scouting party north to reconnoiter the land they hoped to claim for their own. The scouts returned with glowing descriptions of the fertility of the Promised Land. But they also reported very realistically that the land was not going to drop into their laps like a ripe fig. The inhabitants were stalwart citizens and their stoutly fortified towns indicated that they had no intention of handing them over to invaders as poorly equipped as were the Israelites. Still, Josue and Caleb, men of deep faith, insisted that no obstacles were too great for a people that had Yahweh on its side. The people, however, alarmed by reports of the enemy's strength, decided to be "practical," and when Josue and Caleb continued to exhort them to go on with faith in Yahweh, they threatened to stone them on the spot. The Lord was on the point of abandoning them when Moses interceded for them and saved the day. But Yahweh announced that none of the recalcitrants would enter the Promised Land, and that they would all have to spend forty years more in the Sinai wasteland. Perversely, they then decided to attack, but suffered a crushing defeat.

The period which followed is often referred to as the "Wandering in the Desert." This is rather misleading; it brings to mind a picture of the whole immense crowd milling about aimlessly all over the peninsula. Actually they seem to have settled down at Cades, just south of the Negeb. This became their base of operations for the next forty years or so. It was by no means a sterile period. Their quasi-sedentary situation marked a transition from nomadism to agriculture and husbandry, and the new conditions occasioned a further development of their legislation. Administration assumed a more fixed pattern, and the liturgy of the Tabernacle underwent a progressive evolution. But all were aware that it was only a temporary situation and looked forward eagerly to the day when Yahweh would permit them to march on the Promised Land.

Finally Moses gave the long-awaited signal and they moved out of Cades with high hopes. During the past generation they had become a much more homogeneous group than they had been hitherto. This homogeneity was far from perfect, but it was basically solid. Their rugged outdoor life in a forbidding terrain had toughened them up; periodic skirmishes had given them some valuable military experience and, all things considered, they had become a force to be reckoned with. Among other things, they had learned from bitter experience that a frontal attack on the Negeb was out of the question, and so Moses decided on a flanking movement. This called for marching around the southern end of the Dead Sea, then north through Transjordan, and finally west across the Jordan into Chanaan.

It was a long march and the new generation proved as adept at grumbling as their fathers had been. Yahweh had to punish them by sending a swarm of scorpions into the camp. Moses healed the stricken by asking them to look with faith on a bronze serpent fixed to a pole. Since there was obviously no proportion between the remedy and the cure, they would know that it was their faith in Yahweh, so expressed, that healed them. Even Moses, after all these years, incurred the displeasure of Yahweh, who informed him as a result that he would indeed be privileged to see the Promised Land but would never enter it. It seems that the people were suffering from thirst and the Lord told Moses to strike a rock with his staff; water would gush forth in abundance. Moses obeyed, but turned what should have been an impressive display of Yahweh's power and loving kindness into an occasion to give the people a bitter tongue-lashing. He thus degraded a divinely glorious event into a wretchedly human scene. And God who, in His justice, is no respecter of persons, simply could not look the other way.

Internal difficulties were matched by external ones. The king of Edom flatly refused to let them pass through his territory. This necessitated a long detour to the south before they could head north once more along the western border of Edom. Deeming it advisable to avoid a conflict with Moab, Edom's northern neighbor, they filed through the arid gully called the Brook Zered, which formed the boundary between Edom and Moab. After a short rest at the River Arnon, they moved into the home stretch. Victories over the forces of kings Sehon and Og gave them virtual control of practically all of Transjordan, and a great deal of confidence in the bargain. They were on the threshold of the Promised Land; the next step was to establish a bridgehead on the western shore of the Jordan. But on the eve of this momentous step in the history of his people Moses died, but not before he had glimpsed, through tear-misted eyes, the land of his dreams from the summit of Mt. Nebo. He had carried out his commission admirably. Now younger and stouter hearts and hands were needed.

The command passed into the hands of Moses' capable lieutenant, Josue. The general political situation was in his favor, and he took advantage of it. The great empires were all in a state of either decadence or emergence, with troubles of their own to keep them occupied on the home front. The native Chanaanites were hopelessly split into a number of little "city-states" which, though strongly fortified, lacked the staying power which some sort of federation would have given them. The Lord of history had picked the propitious moment for His children to come home. Not that they were able simply to walk in the side door and ask the present tenants to vacate the premises quietly. Just across the Jordan were several strongly fortified towns, and the key to their capture lay in the defeat of the one nearest the river: Jericho. With the timely help of a providential landslide which dammed up the waters of the Jordan for several hours, Josue led his forces across the river and stood, at long last, on the sacred soil which Jacob and his family had left almost four hundred years before.

The Book of Josue contains some of the oldest and most authentic historical documentation in the Bible, but its editor has arranged the data according to a plan which is just a bit too pat. It gives the impression that the Israelites simply swept through the country chalking up victory after victory and then settled down to a division of the land among the twelve tribes. This is basically true but needs to be balanced off by the more realistic picture painted in the Book of Judges. At any rate, thanks to the timely intervention of Yahweh (an opportune earthquake, common in that area, would have brought the massive walls tumbling down), Josue took Jericho. The capture of other key towns in the sector followed. The defeat of a coalition of five Ammorite kings gave the Israelites a measure of control in the south, and the victory over Jabin and his allies brought the north fairy well under their power. Interestingly enough, there is no record of a campaign in the central mountain region, and yet it was apparently in their hands. It has been suggested, and with a good degree of probability, that this area was already settled by kinsfolk of the Israelites, descendants of Jacob who had not gone down to Egypt or who had left from time to time during the sojourn there and had quietly established themselves in central Chanaan.

In any event, Josue's campaign was eminently successful. The Israelites had a firm grip on the land which Yahweh had promised to give them. Under Josue's strong leadership, and with Gilgal (in the Jordan valley not far from Jericho) as a military and religious center, they were able to maintain that unity which alone assures a people's strength. But when the only partly-won land was partitioned among the twelve tribes and Josue had died, that unity was in grave peril. They had taken only enough strategic posts to give them token mastery of the country. Many towns and much valuable farmland still lay in Chanaanite hands, and the Israelites had made hardly a move in the direction of the rich coastal plain. Consequently their military position was still shaky and their proximity to the pagan Chanaanites still living about them presented an even greater peril. The temptation to abandon Yahweh in favor of the more "practical" religion of their neighbors was strong and constant, and many succumbed to that temptation.

This was the situation at the beginning of the period of the Judges. Without a political capital and lacking strong central leadership, they ran the very real risk of being assimilated gradually into the native population. Had this happened, they would have lost their national and religious identity, and the sublime destiny which God had assigned them in human history would have been cancelled out. But He would not allow this to happen. The twelve tribes still maintained a sort of unity. The covenant was solemnly renewed from time to time and the Law went on developing to meet new circumstances. There were shrines here and there throughout the country where He was officially worshiped, and Silo in particular became a popular center of pilgrimage. For here was kept the Ark of the Covenant with the tablets of the Law, that Law which formed the basis of the alliance between God and His people.

The situation, then, was not rosy, but neither was it desperate. For Yahweh was a jealous God, and He would take steps to protect His people, even from themselves. How much they needed this protection the Book of Judges makes shockingly clear. Anarchy, fierce independence, superstition, crime, and disaster muddy its pages, and only a periodically reappearing ray of hope keeps this darkness from settling into a murky gloom. The bearers of this hope are a group of men called Judges. The title does not have the juridical connotations which it has today; in the context of the Bible it signifies rather liberators or saviors. These men carried out their work, not by due process of law, but by physical prowess, military cunning, shrewdness, resourcefulness. They were local heroes who rose to the occasion when one or more of the tribes was threatened by a strong enemy.

When the tribes settled in their respective territories, they lost much of the strength their initial unity had given them. Individually they were a tempting prey for marauding bands of Midianites and Ammonites from the east, for the ambitious Philistines who had but recently invaded Chanaan by way of the Mediterranean, and for their Chanaanite neighbors. But each time disaster threatened, they were forced to an awareness of their helplessness without Yahweh. They turned back to Him for help and He responded by raising up a man who could handle the situation.

Some of these heroes are hardly mentioned while others are given quite a bit of attention, like Othoniel, Aod, Debbora and Barac, Gedeon and Abimelech, Jephte, and Samson. They were men of their times and their times were crude, often savage. But they served Yahweh's immediate purpose, and His choice of them for the task at hand by no means implies His sanction of their moral shortcomings. It was really He who was the Liberator; they just happened to be handy instruments. They operated locally for the most part, working for the benefit of one tribe or a small group of tribes. Only one or two attempted to exercise authority over all the Israelites, and they failed miserably. But as time went on, the people began to realize that security and progress would be theirs only if they joined together under one strong leader. Pressure was increasing on all sides, and they were tired of escaping from peril after peril by the skin of their teeth.

The Philistines especially, formidable warriors with superior weapons, were attacking more and more insistently. There is a note of dire foreboding in the fact that the last of the Judges, the mighty Samson, died in blind rage and frustration as their captive. It was time for a change in national policy, and the man whom an ever-active Providence selected as the agent of that change was Samuel, judge and prophet. Under him the nation was to become a kingdom, thus setting the stage for the establishment of the Kingdom of God when the King of Kings would be born of Israel's royal line and claim the whole world for His realm.

VI

THE KINGDOM OF DAVID

The Period of the Judges had lasted about one hundred and fifty years, and a wild, troubled, period it had been. In many ways it was like our own pioneer days, when small bands of settlers struggled to eke out an existence in an untamed land. The Israelites had to fight off Midianites and Ammonites; our pioneers had to defend themselves against Apaches and Comanches. In both eras lawlessness was rampant, and when law was needed men took it into their own hands, resenting the intrusion of officialdom. But in those far-off days, as in our own nineteenth century, people began to sense the futility of independent action and to realize the advantages of a strong, established union.

It was about the middle of the eleventh century B.C. that God raised up the man who would forge the union needed by the Israelites. His task was extremely delicate. The traditional rivalry among the several tribes, especially between Ephraim in the north and Juda in the south, had fostered an enervating disunity. The Israelites woke up one fine morning and discovered to their horror that the Philistines were camped right on their doorsteps. Too late, they put up a common defense. In the bloody battle of Aphec they were slashed to pieces by a well-organized foe who captured even the Ark of the Covenant. All hope seemed lost. The invaders put up fortresses throughout the commanding mountain country, sacked the shrine at Silo, and confiscated what weapons the Israelites had.

Against this dismal background Samuel grew to manhood. Remarkably gifted, he was already in his prime when the battle of Aphec squelched the independence of his little nation. His mother, in gratitude for his birth, had put him at the service of the priests at Silo, and from there his reputation for dependability, integrity, and nobility of character had spread far and wide. But he was especially esteemed as a prophet, a true man of God, one who knew the divine will and could make it known with sureness. The people's confidence in him grew apace. Courageously, then, he embarked on the arduous work of reconstruction. On his annual tours of the country he instilled a desire for union in the hearts of his compatriots. He neutralized, at least temporarily, the divisive rivalry among the tribes, especially by drawing the powerful southern tribe of Juda into the national orbit. As a consequence of his dedicated activity, Israel grew in unity and strength, and when the hour struck, the Israelites set the Philistines back on their heels and had their Promised Land pretty much to themselves once more.

By far his most significant accomplishment was the development of a unified national consciousness among the people. He put the final touches to the political evolution which was to substitute for the enervating separatism of the individual tribes a national union under one head endowed with stable power. Equally important: being himself a prophet, he established alongside the soon-to-emerge secular authority the counterforce of a religious and prophetical ministry. In a nation like Israel there could be but one supreme authority: God. There was no room for an all-powerful king who recognized no authority above his own. This apparent conflict of authority — Yahweh versus a human king — gave Samuel pause when the representatives of the tribes asked him to pick a man to be their king. God enlightened him to resolve the conflict and sanctioned the choice of Saul as the first king of Israel. The latter carried out his immediate duties with distinction, but in the end he turned out to be one of the most tragic figures in all of human history.

Saul came from the tribe of Benjamin; his father was a fairly comfortably fixed landowner. One day around the year 1030 B.C. the young man went looking for some donkeys which had strayed from the property and, on the advice of a hired hand he had taken along, went to Samuel for help in finding them. It was on this occasion that Yahweh prompted His prophet to anoint him as king. The people subsequently sanctioned this private anointing in a general assembly. They found their first king quite imposing. The sacred text takes pains to point out that he stood head and shoulders above all his subjects. But he was not just a big strong farm boy. He got his administration off to a brilliant start by launching a vigorous and generally successful campaign against the still entrenched Philistines.

The career so promisingly begun was to end dismally. Saul disregarded the orders of Samuel, who was the real power behind the throne and the representative of the Lord. He informed the king in no uncertain terms that Yahweh had rejected him. This falling out with Samuel embittered Saul's very existence. He became morbidly melancholy and fell into dark moods of brooding depression. A young shepherd of Bethlehem named David, who had quite a reputation as a harpist, was called in to cheer up the king with some relaxing music. For a while this therapy worked well and the king became quite fond of his young minstrel. But after the latter's victorious duel with Goliath, when the king heard the people acclaiming David in marked preference to himself, his neurotic tendencies reasserted themselves. He became madly jealous of David and made several frenzied attempts on his life. There was nothing for David to do but flee. Shortly thereafter the hapless Saul met the Philistines in battle on the Plain of Esdraelon. His army was crushed and thrown back towards the heights of Mt. Gelboe. Preferring death to dishonor, he took his own life. Thus ended the truly tragic career of Israel's first king.

It was quite different with his successor, David. He was the darling of his people and became the ideal king of Israel, the one to whom future ages looked back with a deep sigh. So much did they idolize him, in fact, that when divinely inspired hopes for a Messiah took definite shape, those hopes were expressed in terms of the Davidic ideal. The Messiah would be no less than another David. And in truth, the king did deserve this love and admiration, in spite of his frankly chronicled faults.

For some time after escaping from the dangerous presence of the unbalanced Saul, he led a sort of Robin Hood existence with a band of faithful followers. His prestige, already great at the court of Saul, increased during these years. He had been designated by Samuel as Saul's successor, and immediately after the king's death he was proclaimed king at Hebron by the members of his own tribe of Juda. As might have been expected, the northern tribes were reluctant to accept another southerner as king. It took them more than seven years to admit that, southerner or not, David was a man they simply could not refuse to have as their ruler. Cheerful, devout, intelligent, clever, strong, of irresistible personal charm, he was a prince after the heart of the people. They became one under his scepter, and under his strong rule the little nation scaled hitherto undreamed of heights. Not only did it become a secure and prosperous country; it stretched out to almost imperial proportions. It had been a hard, bitter, embattled trek, but Israel had finally arrived!

King David's reign lasted from 1010 to 970, about forty years. In spite of all the brilliant accomplishments of these years, they were not easy. It took the new king more than seven years to win the support of the northern tribes, and when unity had been finally achieved, his work was only begun. The Philistines were still in control of large sections of the country; their victory over Saul and their resultant control of the strategically important Plain of Esdraelon had split the country in two, from west to east. David's first task was to rid his territory of this thorn in the side. So successful was he that he not only pushed them out of his country but even won a measure of control over theirs. In fact, from this time on the Philistines gradually faded out of the picture as an ethnic unit and ended by being absorbed into neighboring groups. But they left a lasting memorial in the name later given the country: Palestine, land of the Philistines. Outside the limits of Israel, Ammonites, Arameans, and Moabites soon found that they had met their match in David.

All that remained in matters military was a mop-up operation on small pockets of Chanaanites still walled-up in their miniature mountain fortresses. One particularly stubborn posi-

tion, from which Israelite attacks had been beaten off since
the days of Josue, finally fell to the indomitable David. It became "his" city, the City of David: Jerusalem. The fact that it
had withstood persistent attacks for so long is a good indication
of its military value. It is unusually well protected by nature,
and its choice as a national capital speaks volumes for David's
shrewdness. But there was more than just the military angle.
Situated on the border separating north and south, it symbolized
and strengthened the shaky unity now existing between the two.

The City of David became the City of God as well. The king
had the Ark of the Covenant brought with great pomp to the
new capital, which thus became the religious as well as the
political center of the nation. A rich liturgy was not long in developing, now that circumstances favored it, and Yahweh was
worshiped in grand style around the symbol of His presence, the
Tabernacle. This "official" worship did not immediately sup-
plant that of the popular shrines throughout the country, but
it certainly overshadowed it.

. Israel seemed to come of age overnight — too quickly, really,
for its own good. The old rivalries among the tribes could not
be snuffed out just like that! The principle of unity which held
them together temporarily was the personal power and prestige
of David. When this began to wane, cracks appeared in the
structure he had so laboriously erected. The second half of his
reign was marred by a succession of misfortunes, misfortunes
arising from his own human weakness and from the passionate
ambitions of his sons.

His downward glide began with his adultery with Bethsabee, his pretty next-door neighbor. This was a heinous enough
crime, but he aggravated it by having her husband, a soldier
doggedly devoted to him, put in the front line of battle, where
he would be sure to meet death — and did. It must be said to
David's credit, however, that when the prophet Nathan took
him to task he repented sincerely and did penance with really
touching humility. The baby who resulted from this illicit union
lived only a week. Then the king's eldest son, Amnon, con-

ceived a violent passion for his own half-sister, Thamar. He ended by violating her. Her brother Absalom had Amnon murdered and took to the hills. David let him come back after a few years and he showed his gratitude by organizing a revolt against his father. A battle ensued in which David's general Joab made quick work of Absalom and broke the king's heart. With Absalom out of the way, his brother Adonias staked his claim to the throne. But Bethsabee, who had become David's rightful wife and had borne Solomon to him, had obtained for her son the right of succession. The prophet Nathan was on her side, and she had Solomon on the throne even before David was dead.

David was undoubtedly the greatest of the kings of Israel. An always victorious soldier and statesman, he was also a sincere and enthusiastic "servant of Yahweh" who contributed, to the limit of his means, to the development of the cult of his God. Nevertheless, he was not unscathed by the customs of his times, as his sins attest. But these ugly shadows on his character did not eclipse the sparkle of his personality or the brilliance of his basic goodness, and in the writings of later biblical authors we meet him as the ideal king.

David, the able warrior king, had succeeded in suppressing all of Israel's enemies. Solomon, who ascended the throne in 970, profited by the situation to build up his realm from within. His very name describes his reign: it is derived from the Hebrew word for peace: *shalom*. He was admirably fitted for the work which faced him. A wizard at administration, his astuteness in this field won for him an imperishable renown for wisdom. Under his direction a united Israel reached the peak of its glory. But for all his wisdom he was limited in vision, and the means he employed to develop his country, while immediately and spectacularly successful, eventually boomeranged and created a situation little short of ruinous.

Solomon was not a soldier; fortunately for him, he did not have to play at being one. He lacked his warm-hearted father's sincere feeling for his people; on the contrary, he alienated them slowly but surely. For all his pompous declarations of loyalty to Yahweh, for all his showy supplications for wisdom in the government of his people, he was not what one would call a godly king.

Solomon the Magnificent was an administrator, a builder, and a businessman. His own palace was the last word in oriental luxury, and the temple, which replaced the portable tabernacle, was the glory of Israel. It became the center of Israel's religious life, the proud symbol of the true religion, the official locale for the worship of Yahweh. At the same time, however, he erected shrines to pagan gods for the convenience of his non-Israelite concubines.

On the administrative level, the king divided the country into twelve districts and appointed men to run them, thus giving birth to a bureaucracy. He established diplomatic relations with foreign countries — his marriage to the daughter of the pharao of Egypt was a stroke of genius — and instituted a flourishing program of international trade. While there was little danger of foreign invasion during his reign, he was wise enough to carry out an extensive preparedness program. Cavalry and chariot detachments manned all the strategic posts, and the garrison at Megiddo, overlooking the vast Plain of Esdraelon, has been excavated and is remarkably intact: hitching posts, stalls, feed troughs are all there for the visitor to see.

But the social evolution of the nation had taken a sharp and dangerous turn with the sudden emergence of a moneyed aristocracy and bureaucracy. Overnight, sharply disparate classes had sprung into being: a few rich and many poor, and the poor were far from happy about the situation. Then to facilitate his building program, the king had conscripted labor gangs — from all the tribes but Juda! Exorbitant taxes were necessary to support himself and his harem in the style to which neighboring potentates were accustomed. The smoldering resentment of the people was ready to blaze into a social crisis of fiery proportions. The old tribal rivalry was flaring up anew; the northerners balked at being practically enslaved by a Judean king who made no secret of his favoritism among members of his own tribe. Around the twenty-fourth year of his reign, an Ephraimite by the name of Jeroboam, with the backing of the prophet Ahias, instigated a rebellion. It failed but he managed to escape to Egypt, there to bide his time.

This was an ominous cloud on the horizon. It cast a disturbing shadow on the glitter of the capital of the United Kingdom, and the lightning which would soon flash from it would split that kingdom in two and begin a process of disintegration destined to end in the ruin of both North and South. Solomon had brought Israel to the heights, but in such a way as to give it its initial push into the depths.

VII

THE KINGDOM DIVIDED

Solomon's son and successor, Roboam, could have preserved the unity of his realm if he had had even a grain of political sense. It would not have been easy, but it was within his power. Instead, his adolescent arrogance infuriated the northern tribes and drove a wedge between them and Juda which was never to be withdrawn. They sent a delegation to him offering their allegiance if only he would relax some of the oppressive measures of his father. His consultors, wise and realistic men, urged him to grant their requests. But his own young crowd, with typical irresponsibility, teased him into an unreasonable attitude of defiance. Not only did he not meet the fair demands of the northern tribes; he rather childishly boasted that if they thought his father had made things difficult for them they were in for a surprise. They hadn't seen anything yet! To this stupidity the North had a ready answer. It formed its own kingdom under Jeroboam; it was known as the Kingdom of Israel, or simply Ephraim, after its most prominent tribe. The southern kingdom, with its capital at Jerusalem, was called Juda.

As kingdoms go, the United Kingdom of Israel had been

tiny — about the size of Vermont — but in its unity it had found strength. Now, split into two very unequal parts, it was vulnerable from without and torn by civil strife within. The northern kingdom included ten of the twelve tribes and consequently far outstripped Juda in territory and population. But its very position was a constant danger. The Hebrews' most formidable enemies usually came from the north, and so the new kingdom lay directly in the path of savage and enterprising armies, armies which would make the Philistines of old look like wooden soldiers. Internally, Israel lacked cohesion. Starting from scratch as it was, it had no stable dynasty, no religious center, and for a long time no capital city worthy of the name.

The southern kingdom, on the other hand, enjoyed the advantage of a smoothly organized administration. Its compact population lived under a glorious dynasty, the house of David, and could look with confidence and pride to a capital which was at one and the same time strong and holy: Jerusalem. As for external threats, it had Israel as a buffer state between it and potential attack from belligerent nations to the north and east. On the south, Egypt posed something of a threat, but not a really serious one, since that once great power had been on the downgrade for the past three centuries. Pharao Sesac did sack the temple and royal palace during the reign of Roboam (932-915), but this was just an isolated foray. The only grave peril came from their own blood brothers, the Israelites of the northern kingdom.

This peril materialized more than once, and the history of the Divided Kingdom was a dismal one for the first fifty years of its existence. It was a period of instability and uneasiness for the North. Three out of every five kings who ascended the throne during this time were assassinated by power-greedy rivals. Confident of its military superiority, the North often attacked the South, but without ever winning a decisive victory.

A new era in the history of Israel and Juda dawned with the reign of Omri (885-874) in the North. He built the fine capital of Samaria and built up a solid economy. A former army general, he realized the futility of the constant attacks on Juda. For one thing, he could see Damascus looming more and more threateningly on the horizon and foresaw the day when the two kingdoms might have to put up a united front or be swept off the map. To strengthen his position still further, he concluded a treaty with the king of Tyre and married his son Achab to the Tyrian princess Jezabel. This may have been astute foreign policy, but it turned out to be a domestic catastrophe, for Jezabel was an idolatrous pagan and managed to act the part very convincingly later on.

. The fruit of this unholy union, Athalia by name, was then given in marriage to Joram, king of Juda. This move drew still tighter the bonds between North and South and the civil war was a thing of the past. The resultant peace brought increased prosperity. The economic situation was sound and the living was easy, at least for the privileged and moneyed classes. But the latter lived luxuriously and scandalously, and not the least scandalous aspect of their behavior was the way they flouted elementary social justice and ground the poor under heel. In a word, God's people were becoming as vicious and worldly as the pagans whose civilization they were trying so hard to ape. Commercial and social relations with foreigners were becoming commonplace, and along with the latters' merchandise and women came the false gods which should have been an abomination to the worshipers of the one true God.

A bloody coup engineered by Jehu in 843 brought a savagely violent end to the house of Omri. The new era reached its peak during the reign of Jeroboam II (785-745). His long and prosperous reign was matched in the South by that of Ozias, also called Azarias (790-739). Both kingdoms were at peace and secure from threat of foreign invasion. True, Assyria had forced Jehu to pay annual tribute, but there was at the moment a lull in her rise to imperial domination, and Israel and Juda took advantage of the respite to build up and enjoy a strong economy. From the latter point of view, both kingdoms were at their peak. But again it was a one-sided prosperity, and never had social injustice been so unfeelingly cruel. Religion was a sham, a cover-up for vice and licentiousness. The people practiced religion, to be sure, in the sense that they went through the motions of sacrifice and ritual. But they were empty motions, motions made in the superstitious hope that they would keep Yahweh happy regardless of the dispositions of the ones who made them.

After the long reign of Jeroboam II, a series of royal assassinations followed until Manahem, himself an assassin, succeeded in stabilizing the ship of state for about ten years. His death was the signal for more anarchy. His son and successor Phaceia was cut down after a reign of hardly two years. His murderer, Phacee, instituted a foreign policy which was to have a disturbing effect on the kingdom of Juda. He entered into a coalition of kings who were sick and tired of paying tribute to Assyria and had decided to throw off the yoke. The new king of Juda, Achaz (735-720) had too much respect for the military might of Assyria to risk his neck in any such madcap venture and refused to join the alliance. Thereupon, either to force his hand or to steal his resources, King Rasin of Damascus and Phacee of Israel ganged up on him. This was the so-called Syro-Ephraimitic War. It gets its name from the two nations which attacked Juda: Syria and Israel, often called Ephraim, the tribe within whose borders the capital city of Samaria was situated. Adding insult to injury, Achaz turned to the archenemy for help, and the ambitious Assyrian monarch, Theglathphalasar, was delighted at the opportunity to mop up the troublesome little Mediterranean states. His armies marched through northern Israel, leaving devastation in their wake. Kings Rasin and Phacee pulled out of Juda and took to their heels. The once proud northern kingdom was reduced to a satellite of Assyria. Phacee was assassinated by one Osee, who ascended the throne as a puppet of Theglathphalasar. He was destined to be the last king of Israel.

When the mighty Assyrian monarch died he left his empire to his son Salmanasar V (727-723). The king of Tyre decided to assert his independence and Osee of Israel, too, made up his mind that he had had enough of being a puppet on an Assyrian string. Salmanasar brought them both back into line in short order, but no sooner had he returned home than Egypt, still hoping to recapture some of her past glory, started negotiations with the disenchanted little Mediterranean states with an eye to forming a coalition against Assyria. Osee, who apparently just couldn't learn, joined the pro-Egyptian forces.

We are not told how it happened, but Salmanasar had Osee taken prisoner. Then, fed up with the backsliding and intrigue of Israel, he decided to crush it out of existence. He started the siege of Samaria in 725. Amazingly, the city held out for three years. In fact, Salmanasar did not live to complete its capture. But his successor, the powerful Sargon II, was in on the finish. No puppet king was set up this time; an Assyrian governor took over, and to prevent further trouble, the cream of the population, to the number of 27,290, was cruelly uprooted and deported. Thus, in 722 B.C., the ten tribes which had made up the northern kingdom stumbled out of the pages of history, never to be heard from again. The Assyrians, in keeping with their usual policy, brought in deportees from other vanquished lands to substitute for the banished Israelites. Thus Samaria was peopled with pagan foreigners who gradually formed an amalgam with the wretched Israelites who had been left behind. This is the origin of the Samaritans whom we meet in later Jewish history and in the gospels. The Jews despised them, a hybrid race made up of an admixture of Hebrew and Gentile blood of all sorts. And future clashes between the two only served to embitter this basic antagonism.

The little kingdom of Juda now stood as a tiny isle in a sea of belligerent paganism. Ezechias, son of Achaz, became king in 727, and no son could have been more unlike the father who begot him. He was, to begin with, solidly pious and instituted a thorough religious reform. This religious spirit guided his political administration, and the country enjoyed a long spell of blessed peace as a result. True, he had to pay tribute to

Assyria, but it was a small enough price to pay for the peace, prosperity, and religious freedom it ensured. There were serious temptations to adopt a different policy, however.

The Mideast was seething with unrest. When Salmanasar died, a power which had lain dormant for quite a while decided to reassert itself. That power was Babylon, and it found strong leadership in the Chaldean Merodac-Baladan II. He managed to maintain his independence for the next twelve years. His boldness was infectious, and the little Mediterranean states, again with the shaky backing of Egypt, formed an anti-Assyrian league. But Sargon, who had completed the siege of Samaria, made short work of the coalition. Fortunately Ezechias, at the advice of the prophet Isaias, had stayed out of the league. And again in 711 the same situation arose with Ezechias again resisting the temptation to take advantage of it. But when Sargon died, hopes rose throughout the empire. It was about this time that Ezechias fell seriously ill, and while he was convalescing Merodac-Baladan sent a delegation to Jerusalem and won the king's support. Sennacherib, the new ruler of Assyria, reacted with alacrity. He defeated Merodac-Baladan and then turned his attention to the recalcitrant states in the west. He had beaten them all into submission and was about to attack Juda when trouble in the east diverted his attention. But it was only a temporary reprieve. He returned and laid siege to Jerusalem. The city was saved only because a plague decimated the Assyrian army, forcing it to retire weakly from the field and make its wobbly way home.

The half-century following Ezechias' death in 693 would best be passed over in silence. Manasses, son of Ezechias, was the lowest of the low. His grandfather Achaz had been bad enough, but not even he had been so utterly perverse as was this traitor to the divine trust. His son and successor, Amon, was assassinated before he could do any more damage. He was apparently a chip off the old block, but a reign of about one year (638) gave him little chance to prove it. His sudden departure put an eight-year-old boy on the throne. Since he was unable to govern personally, his affairs were conducted by regents, and of this period of his career we know very little. But Josias was to grow up to become one of the glories of his people. He undertook a methodical cleanup of the religious situation. Centralizing worship in the temple, he tore down the flourishing idolatrous shrines and tried in general to give the people the kind of religion Yahweh wanted them to have, a religion centered in the one true God and both demanding and fostering high moral ideals in every department of life.

The events which were taking place outside of Palestine during this time were literally world-shaking. The dreaded empire of Assyria was on the way out. Babylon, which had been a constant thorn in its side, had finally come into its own, and a new balance of power was forming. Allied with the Babylonians were the warlike Medes to the east; together they made up a formidable axis. Egypt, ever shifty, joined forces with the embattled Assyrians. But nothing could stop the Babylonian juggernaut. In 614 it crushed the city of Assur, and in 612, after an unimaginably fierce battle, Niniveh, the glittering capital of Assyria, crumbled in defeat. What was left of the Assyrian forces made their way to Harran. Chased out of there two years later, they retreated to Carchemish, a strategic spot on the upper Euphrates. It was at this juncture that Pharao Nechao of Egypt decided to help his beleaguered ally. To reach Carchemish he had to pass through Juda. Josias, taking a dim view of this unwarranted encroachment on his territory, intercepted the Egyptian army in the plain of Megiddo. It was his last heroic act; he was killed in the battle which ensued (609), much to the detriment of the kingdom of Juda.

The victorious pharao proceeded to exercise a little tyranny of his own. After three months he summarily deposed Joachaz, son and successor of Josias. In his stead he appointed another son of the dead king, Joakim, who was known for his Egyptophile tendencies. He then went on his way to Carchemish, but in the battle which took place there in 605, the Babylonian Nabuchodonosor crushed irrevocably all hopes for Assyrian survival. A new era had begun. It was a dismal era, eventually the most dismal of eras. Under Joakim's rule idolatrous practices began to mushroom once more. The reform undertaken by Josias had not had time to sink roots deep in the hearts of the people and, as soon as its restraints were lifted, they went back to their old ways. At the same time, his foreign policy was most unintelligent. Anyone with any knowledge of the situation should have realized that Nabuchodonosor could not be tampered with, that patient submission was the only sensible policy at the moment. But Pharao Nechao, still smarting from the defeat he had suffered at Carchemish, was lobbying for revolt against Babylon. There was a strong pro-Egyptian faction in Jerusalem; the king himself had marked leanings in that direction, and about 601 he revolted. Nabuchodonosor didn't deign to retaliate personally. Instead he gave Israel's neighbors — Syrians, Moabites, and Ammonites — the green light to raid Juda. Joakim succeeded in fighting them off and Nabuchodonosor sent his own troops to teach the upstart a lesson.

Death snatched Joakim from the ignominy of defeat; he passed away while the city's defenses were being strengthened. His son Jechonias (usually called Joachin) succeeded him and had to bear the brunt of the attack. In 598 Nabuchodonosor came in person to take over, and it wasn't long before the city fell. The young king, after a reign of just three months, was hustled off into exile with his mother, his wives, his administrators, and the cream of the population. Nabuchodonosor stripped the capital of its wealth and set up Joachin's uncle Matthanias (third son of Josias) as king, changing his name to Sedecias.

The new king, destined to be the last king of Juda, was an unfortunate weakling. To begin with, he was little more than a puppet of Nabuchodonosor, but he lacked even the strength to hold on to the end of the Babylonian string. In 588 he entered into a coalition against his overlord and thus signed his country's death warrant. Early in that same year a powerful Babylonian army encircled Jerusalem and began the siege which was to end in the city's fall. The end came in the summer of 587. After a siege of eighteen months the Babylonians succeeded in breaking through the walls of Jerusalem. The exhausted defenders, emaciated from lack of food and sleep, offered no further resistance. The people were led off into exile and their proud city was put to the torch. The temple, the royal palace, everything was reduced to smoldering rubble, and the stout walls which had held off the enemy for a year and a half were pulverized by Babylonian demolition crews. Juda was no more. The Babylonian Captivity had begun.

VIII

THE PROPHETS AND THEIR MESSAGE

Throughout the history of His people, God kept in touch with them through selected representatives known as prophets, men specially chosen and enlightened to make His will known. They thus made up one of the most important and influential institutions in the Old Testament. Soon after the Hebrews became a nation seers turned up in their history. Of course, the very instrument of their national formation, Moses, was a prophet — in fact, *the* prophet — but in a far more profound sense than were those early seers, as we shall point out shortly. There were, in general, two classes of seers in the days of Israel's infancy. There was the type to whom one went to "consult Yahweh." They were usually, but not always, priests, men especially well equipped to make God's will known on various matters. Then there was the type whose "prophesying" strikes us as quite bizarre. They seem to have lived in groups and to have given themselves up frequently to a rather frenzied ecstasy, usually induced by music and manifesting itself in energetic dancing and gyrations of all sorts.

The word "prophet" or "prophecy" almost automatically

suggests someone or something connected with the prediction of a future event. So spectacular was this element in the work of the prophets that it overshadowed in the popular mind what were actually more basic elements, and the notion of prophecy became accordingly restricted in everyday speech. In fact, however, the prediction of things to come is not of the essence of biblical prophecy. Fundamentally, a prophet was one who spoke for or on behalf of God, a man with a message from heaven (from the Greek *pro,* for, and *phanai,* to speak). Their message did often deal with threats of future punishment or promises of future blessings, but it was the message which mattered, whether it concerned things past or present or yet to come.

, As salvation history moved on, there appeared those prophets who are more familiar to us than the "seers" of the early days. It is fairly easy to separate them into two classes: the *professional* prophets and the *vocational* prophets. The former group bears some resemblance to those strange associations of seers which flourished in the early days. But the resemblance is far from complete. The authentic professional prophets were men who, of their own choice, held themselves in readiness to do God's bidding — specifically, to make His will known to the people. They usually attached themselves to some great figure like Elias or Eliseus and were known as "sons of the prophets."

Human nature being what it is, some of these men were mere quacks and charlatans, willing to say anything they thought would please a client, especially if they suspected that the client would greet the good news with a generous tip. These were the "false prophets" who caused God's authentic spokesmen no end of trouble (see Jer. 28). In general, however, they were honest and distinterested, and Yahweh often made use of their generous services. But the most noble and influential representatives of the prophetic office were the *vocational* prophets. As their name indicates, they became prophets not on their own initiative, but as the result of a special vocation or call from Yahweh. Moses was the first of this noble line, and the Bible has recorded the names of many others: Samuel, Gad, Nathan, Ahias, Elias, and

Eliseus are among the better known. Still others have remained nameless and are referred to simply as "men of God." Although the exploits of all these men are described more or less fully in the sacred pages, especially in the books of Samuel and Kings, they themselves left nothing in writing, as far as we know. But several true vocational prophets have had their words preserved for posterity in what are called the Prophetic Books of the Bible. They are the best known of all, these so-called *writing* prophets. Their impact on sacred history, their contribution to man's knowledge of God and of himself, and their influence on our literature and general culture would be very difficult to estimate.

In sum, then, the prophets were essentially men called by God to speak for Him, to be His champions in a world all too prone to forget Him and to sink into a blind secularism. Let the world say what it might, devise this or that course of action, they could stand up fearlessly and proclaim with supreme confidence: "Thus says the Lord!" What was the origin of this unshakable conviction of theirs? We cannot be so naïve as to imagine the Holy Spirit in the form of a dove perched on a prophet's shoulder, whispering heavenly knowledge into his ear. But we should be able to explain at least partially the process which enabled these men to say confidently and without the slightest hesitation: "Thus says the Lord!"

Each of the prophets seems to have been favored, at the beginning of his career, with an extraordinary religious experience which shook him to the depths of his soul and left him a changed man, a man of God. A familiar example of this would be the vision of St. Paul on the road to Damascus, that profound encounter with Jesus which transformed him on the spot from a fire-breathing ravager of Christ's infant Church into an apostle whose indefatigable zeal drove him all over the world of his day to win souls for the Savior. This "inaugural vision" of his is strikingly analogous to those of the prophets. See, for instance, Is. 6; Jer. 1:4-10; Ezech. 1-3. The inaugural vision of Isaias is especially illustrative. It made the deepest possible impression on him, and his profound realization of Yahweh's holiness colors all his preaching. Any sin, any infidelity to Yahweh, would have made him wince, even under ordinary circumstances, so fine were his sensibilities, so sincere his piety. But now, with this vision of God's unutterable holiness burning always brightly before him, the sins of his people were almost unbearable. Indeed, his first reaction to the vision was an almost crushing awareness of his own unworthiness. To reassure him, God ordered one of the angels to take a red hot coal from the altar of incense and press it to the prophet's lips as a symbol of his purification. Heartened and emboldened by this gesture, Isaias volunteered to act as Yahweh's spokesman, to champion his cause in a sinful world.

As a result of such an ineffable encounter, the prophet looked at the world with new eyes, with the eyes of God. In this light, people and events took on new color, new meaning. They were perceived, not just in themselves, not just within the narrow framework of time and space, but within the broad framework of the divine plan of salvation. History ceased for them to be merely historical; it became historic, charged with eternal significance. The history of the Chosen People, past and present, came into new, sharper focus, and it was this picture of that history which the prophets presented to the world.

We do not ordinarily think of mystics as men of action. The quiet contemplative calm usually associated with heavenly visions suggests rather the unruffled prayerful existence of a cloistered Carmelite or of a Carthusian solitary. But mysticism and action are far from incompatible, and we find them happily wedded in the prophets. These men of God were intensely active, embroiled in human affairs of all sorts. For grace does not destroy nature; it elevates it to a higher plane of operation. The grace of prophecy did not put its recipients in a perpetual trance. Rather it sharpened and deepened their perception and enabled them to take part in the events of history without being distracted by these events from understanding their meaning in the eternal plan of salvation.

They were public figures, vitally concerned with national and international issues, and their precise task was to put those issues in their proper perspective, to help people see them from God's point of view. We have seen how badly this point of view needed clear statement during the centuries when prophecy was at its height, during the period of the decline and dissolution of the Davidic Kingdom. This was an era of constant crisis, a crisis triggered by general infidelity to Yahweh. Material prosperity brought materialistic corruption into Israelite society, and the very men whose office it was to counteract this corruption failed miserably. Indeed, they were among the most pathetic of its victims. Men's hearts grew harder, and their ears became more and more deaf to appeals which God sent through ordinary channels. Drastic, extraordinary measures were called for if anything was to be salvaged from the debris, and God took just such measures: He raised up the prophets.

Amos preached God's justice in the northern kingdom during the days of Jeroboam II, when social injustice of the crassest kind was crying to heaven for vengeance. Osee followed him with his poignant message of God's love for His sinful people, of His reluctance to punish them, of His eagerness to take them back if they would only repent. They did not, and the northern kingdom continued on its way to extinction. Isaias pleaded with Achaz to trust in Yahweh and abandon his mad plan to call upon the Assyrians to help him in the Syro-Ephraimitic War. He counseled the good Ezechias and succeeded in averting disaster after disaster when the king took his inspired advice. Jeremias had the heart-breaking task of trying to keep a line of dissolute kings from taking the steps which led eventually to the Babylonian Exile; his efforts cost him a living martyrdom and eventual death as an exile in Egypt. Ezechiel kept alive the ideals and the hopes of the exiles in Babylonia, staved off their assimilation into a foreign people, and thus preserved a remnant which would eventually return to the Holy Land and continue the process of salvation history.

It would have been bad enough if any nation sank into the

morass of idolatry, conducted domestic affairs with rank injustice to the underprivileged, used wealth and leisure and culture for grossly immoral purposes. But — and this was the fact of paramount importance — *Israel was God's own people,* chosen especially by Him out of all the peoples of the world. They had a vital role assigned to them in the drama of salvation, a drama to be played out on the stage of human history, a drama which was not just play-acting, but very real, terribly real, for on its outcome hung mankind's eternal fate. Israel's history, then, was not just history; it was *salvation history,* the process God chose for the redemption of the world.

In a sense, the Hebrew prophets were the world's first historians. Other nations, it is true, had their chronicles, their records, their accounts of wars won and lost, their stories of heroes national and local. But it was the prophets who first saw the *meaning* of historical events. This "sense of history" was one of the prime characteristics of prophetic inspiration. The prophets' minds were supernaturally illumined to perceive that what seemed on the surface to be isolated episodes of purely local interest and importance were in reality world-shaking events, all of them knit together by a divine purpose and intended to lead to a divine result: man's salvation. Each episode of Israel's history was a step in the realization of the divine plan. If it was not a step forward, it was a step backward and hence a catastrophe, a tragic betrayal of the trust which Yahweh had placed in His people, the instrument of His merciful plan for mankind. The prophets were endowed with a keen realization of the fact that human history had a *definite goal,* that it was not just a purposeless, capricious interplay of uncontrollable forces.

. What was this goal? The ultimate salvation of mankind, surely, but not even the prophets were privileged with a clearly detailed picture of how this would actually work out. They knew with a grace-assured conviction that God was leading men to an era of peace, freedom, happiness, all those things which make up the "good life." This conviction formed the basis of a hope which nothing could shake, not even moral corruption, war, desolation, or exile. No matter how severe the catastrophe, at least a remnant of the people would survive to carry on the work of God, to be channels of His blessings to men. This idea of a remnant is a constant refrain in the prophetic writings, an expression of their undying hope. See Is. 1:9; 4:3; 10:20-22; 11:11-12; Mich. 2:12; 4:7; 5:6-7; 7:18; Soph. 2:9; 3:13; Jer. 23:3; 31:7; Is. 46:3; 65:8; 66:19; Zach. 8:6, 11, 12. It is this hope which has come to be known as messianism, which we shall consider in detail in Chapter X.

IX

FORMATION OF THE OLD TESTAMENT CHURCH

The "Church" of the Old Testament, strictly speaking, was formed at Mt. Sinai, when Yahweh adopted the Israelites as His own special people and entered into a covenant relationship with them. They became a theocracy, a nation ruled by God, a nation with an essentially religious spirit. But in the years that followed, in spite of God's providential guidance, in spite of the fervent pleas and threats of His prophets, a steadily encroaching paganism smothered that spirit and led to the dissolution of the nation. It took the fires of the Babylonian Captivity to purge away the dross and transform the nation into a church.

"Captivity" has such a sinister ring to it. We are inclined to conjure up pictures of concentration camps, slave labor, chain gangs, eventual extermination. In actual fact, it was no picnic, especially at first, but we must not let our imaginations run away with us. The exiles were, for the most part, the upper crust of Judean society, intelligent, clever, sensitive. To get to Babylon they had to march some 1200 miles under a blistering sun, driven along like immense herds of cattle; and after they had passed along their painful way, many a skeleton lay gaunt and bleak, mute testimony to the rigors of the march and to the hungry efficiency of the ever-circling vultures.

After such a trek as this, arrival at their destination must have seemed almost a relief. The country of their destination was not at all unpleasant. Situated between the great Tigris and Euphrates rivers and well watered by an ingenious system of irrigation canals, it was, for the most part, fresh and green and pretty. And Babylon itself! They had thought Jerusalem a wonder city, with its temple and palaces and handsome homes. Alongside of Babylon it paled into insignificance. Here was a city into which had poured the wealth of conquered nation after conquered nation. It was actually considered one of the wonders of the world, with its massive walls and buildings of brick adorned with figures in glazed and tinted clay, its hanging gardens, its fountains and pools. The exiles were cultured men and women, with an acquired taste for the finer things in life, and they were deeply impressed. And their impressions were going to color their lives, affect their attitudes, and play, consequently, an important part in the destiny of God's people.

Cultured or no, they were captives. They were housed in camps — call them concentration camps if you will — and put to work on the many projects which would make Babylon even more of a jewel than it already was. This was, of course, slave labor, but it was not intended to be a permanent situation. Little by little, the exiles were allowed to melt into the permanent population, to find a place of their own in the vast social structure of the empire. Some started little farms to support themselves and their families, but most of them seem to have been attracted by the many opportunities offered in the city, especially in commercial enterprises. A few found their way into governmental positions, and many managed to amass quite a fortune. Thus, after unavoidably difficult beginnings, the Babylonian Captivity tapered off gradually into a not too abnormal round of living. But were the Jews to become Babylonians purely and simply? What was to become of God's plan of salvation in which they, as a people, were to play the major role? Where was the "remnant," the nucleus saved from the catastrophe, the foundation of the new people of God, partners in the New Alliance?

Life in Babylon was bristling with problems for the exiles. At first, of course, their difficulties were the obvious ones: homesickness, lack of material comforts, anxiety about their loved ones left back in Juda, the hardships of forced labor. But there were deeper problems than these, graver, more permanent, more consequential problems. Should they try to stick together as a distinct group or should they, as the ten tribes of the north had done, simply allow themselves to be absorbed into their new surroundings? To some it seemed like a nightmare from which they would soon awake; the exile would soon be over and they would be allowed to return to their homes.

As time went on, it became painfully clear that the nightmare was a reality and that hopes for a quick return were vain indeed. This gave rise to discouragement, and it took an especially dangerous turn. What had become of all their grandiose hopes of days gone by? Yahweh had promised them that they, as His people, would be the salvation of the world. Now look at them! Perhaps Yahweh was not the one true God, after all. From the looks of things, the gods of the Babylonians were much more real and powerful. Of course, it rarely occurred to those who entertained such blasphemous thoughts that it was *they* who had failed Yahweh and not He who had failed them.

In view of such a situation as this, it is one of the most remarkable facts of human history that the exiles, in the main, did not allow themselves to be swallowed up by the inevitable. With hopes of national restoration growing dimmer by the day, they still insisted on remaining a nation apart, Yahweh's nation. They capitalized on the forces which drew them together rather than on those which pulled them asunder. They had quite literally walked a long way together, and the march into exile must have been marked by countless acts of courage, of unselfish heroism, which forged strong bonds of loyalty among them. Together they had shared the same hardships, and class distinctions melted away as priests, government officials, and laborers worked shoulder to shoulder on Babylonian construction projects. Life in the camps had a leveling effect, too: all dressed pretty much alike; everyone's home was quite the same as his neighbor's. Private problems like sickness and injury became community affairs, with everyone showing genuine and practical concern. And, of course, they all shared memories of the same homeland, and common memories tend strongly to draw people together. But above all, it was their religion which made them unique, made them one; and in spite of all the factors at work against that religion, it stood firm. The words of the old prophets still haunted their memories, the beautiful psalms of their liturgy sprang quite naturally to their lips, and as they sang them together in this strange land, they realized their beauty and the lofty purity of their message as they had never realized them before.

As they pondered their religious past, they recognized more and more clearly the fact that, after all, Yahweh's people had been in some discouraging spots before and He had always rescued them in the end. Just their wondrous liberation from apparently hopeless slavery in Egypt centuries before gave a strong basis for hope, and that was merely one of a long series of divine interventions in favor of the Chosen People. So they would be faithful to Him, their only hope. Of course, without the temple, their religion would have to take on a somewhat different external form. Their sacred books became the center about which they rallied. By this time many of them had been edited in writing and others, through constant repetition, were fixed indelibly on prodigious Semitic memories. These books contained their specific national heritage and did a great deal to keep alive their national consciousness. Privately they meditated on them; in groups they gathered together to hear them read and explained. Thus arose that class of men known later as the Scribes, or Doctors of the Law, men who knew the Book well enough to make it known to others in an authoritative way.

Perhaps the most important single figure in the painful

transition from the old order to the new was the prophet Ezechiel. He had been deported in the exile of 598 and so was involved in the transition right from the start, ten years before the final destruction of Jerusalem. He has often been called the father of Judaism, and he has a right to this distinction on several counts. Just the fact that he contributed so mightily to keeping the people together as a distinct national and religious unit when so many forces were at work to pull them apart — that alone would justify giving him this grand title. But his influence was by no means limited to the direct impact he had on his own generation. He had taken the materials of Israel's old traditions and had reworked them, giving them a new direction, a new meaning. His teaching on the transcendent oneness and holiness of Yahweh, on the personal moral responsibility of each individual human being, his view of Israel as a religious community, a "church," rather than as a nation — all of this exerted a profound influence on subsequent Jewish thinking and writing.

In 538 the Persian general Cyrus, who had conquered Babylon the year before, issued a decree permitting the Jews to return to Palestine and to rebuild their temple. The reaction was mixed. Some of the Jews had carved out successful careers for themselves in the land of exile and were quite content to stay right where they were. But they did contribute generously to the work of reconstruction and it was not long before large groups were organized for the trip home. It is impossible to describe in detail the period of reconstruction. Difficulties of all sorts beset the repatriates, and only the efforts of prophets like Aggeus, Zacharias, and Malachias and of strong leaders like Esdras and Nehemias kept the venture from ending as a horrible fiasco. It was Esdras especially who put into practical effect the spirit which had been fermenting during the Babylonian Exile.

These years of estrangement from the land of their fathers had forced the Jews to look at themselves against the backdrop of the world scene, to realize their uniqueness, to evaluate the sacred heritage which was theirs, and to adapt that heritage to conditions which were startlingly new. It was thus that Judaism was born, that way of life which colors every page of the gospels and which, as a result, is so familiar to us all, with its temple, its scribes, its Doctors of the Law, its Synagogues, its Sanhedrin, its High Priests.

What made Judaism so different from the way of life of pre-exilic times, the Jews so different from the Hebrews, the Israelites? Such a change as this is never simple; one cannot point to any one thing and say that it alone accounts for the difference. But of the several factors involved, by far the most significant was the almost exclusively religious character of the new Israel. Before the Exile it had been a monarchy; now it was a "church." The royalty, as a power, had never risen from the ashes of Jerusalem. The priesthood had continued; it had preserved the nation from assimilation and extinction in Babylon; it had formed a new people in the spirit of Ezechiel, its foremost representative; it had guided its return to the fatherland; it now formed the core of the Jewish nation. The Law, the constitution of the reborn state, was the Law of God, the Law of Moses, interpreted, developed, perfected by the priests during the Exile and promulgated solemnly by Esdras, himself a priest.

All hope of political autonomy was apparently abandoned. Zorobabel, who had led the first group of repatriates, Esdras, and Nehemias had all shown perfect obedience to the Persian Empire. Juda was a pitiful little pocket of land, a dot on the empire's map. That it should ever assert its independence against this mighty colossus was simply unthinkable. And so the little country grew in upon itself. Hemmed in by walls of its own building, it became a closed system, and the center of the system was the temple. The Law, which controlled every aspect of life, personal and social, became its dominant preoccupation. It was the subject of discussion, of meditation, of prayer. It had its official interpreters who applied and reapplied its prescriptions to meet all circumstances. All of this led to that isolationism which became such a characteristic trait of Judaism.

This new, exaggerated isolationism was bound to lead to a certain narrow-mindedness in certain quarters, and it did. But the more noble-minded of the Jews never lost their breadth of vision. Their hopes for the age of the Messiah reached out to embrace all men, not just their compatriots. There were clear signs during this period of a real spiritual ferment, an awakening, an intensification which was to bear rich fruit in the years to come. And of course this spiritual awareness, this soulful yearning was a providential part of the preparation for the coming of Him who alone could satisfy such yearning.

There is one institution the mere mention of which makes one think of the Jewish people, of Judaism. That is the synagogue. A distinctive part of the Judaism which took definite form after the Exile, it had come into being during the years in Babylon. Hundreds of miles from the temple, which was a ruin anyway, they had to find some place where they could gather together for divine worship. Soon little congregations, synagogues, were formed. Sacrifice could be offered only at the temple, and this fact necessitated the development of some other form of worship. They settled for what we would call prayer meetings. A passage of the Law would be read, and someone who was equipped for the task would explain it and base an exhortation on it. There would be private prayer and meditation and the recitation or singing of their beloved hymns, the psalms. Even after they had returned from Babylon and had rebuilt the temple, the synagogue endured as an institution. After all, small though Juda was, not everyone could make it to the temple as often as he would like, and the local or neighborhood synagogue filled the need which the people felt for frequent instruction and communal prayer.

The Jews brought back with them something else which was quite new: a new language. Before the Exile, Hebrew had been their national idiom. But another language was spoken in Babylon, and they spent fifty years and more there. A whole new generation had been born in exile, and since they had no idea just when they would be returning to Juda, if ever, they adopted the language of the country in which they would apparently have to make their way through life. That language was Aramaic. It was actually quite close to Hebrew; both were Semitic languages. The Persian Empire, too, had adopted Aramaic as its official language, and so it remained the common means of communication in business, commerce, and government. Thus it was that when our Lord was born some four hundred years later, the language which He learned from the lips of Mary and Joseph, the language in which He trained His disciples and taught His compatriots, was Aramaic.

The period which intervened before His coming is a sort of Dark Ages as far as historical information about the Jews is concerned. Late in the fourth century Alexander the Great displaced the Persians as the ruling world power, and the Jews seem to have taken the turnover in stride. After his death his empire was split among his generals, and Juda was at first under the jurisdiction of the Ptolemies in Egypt. Later it fell under the rule of the Seleucids, whose center of operation was in Syria. It was one of these monarchs, Antiochus Epiphanes, who tried to Hellenize the Jews and touched off the Maccabean revolution. The result of this uprising was the re-establishment of the monarchy in Juda, with descendants of the Maccabees, the so-called Hasmonean Dynasty, on the throne. It was into this dynasty that the Idumean opportunist, Herod the Great, married, and the political stage was set for the coming of the King of Kings.

X

THE EXPECTATION OF A MESSIAH

God in His wisdom revealed His truth, doctrinal and moral, only very gradually, and the sacred books are, in a sense, the record of that progressive revelation. Among the truths so revealed was that concerning the Messiah and His work, the doctrine we call messianism. Now messianism is not a simple concept. In its broadest connotation, it is merely Israel's conviction of its own divinely planned destiny and the hope growing out of that conviction. In its strict meaning, it is the firm hope for the coming of an extraordinarily endowed individual who will lead the people to the perfect realization of that destiny. Centuries of inspired thinking and a long and complex series of historical and psychological factors intervened between the two. And even then, prescinding from the actual fulfillment of these hopes in the coming of Jesus the Christ, the Jews could conceive of the achievement of their destiny apart from the intervention of any such individual. For them, messianism without a Messiah involved no contradiction.

As a matter of fact, however, there was real and discernible progress in the development of the messianic doctrine of the Old Testament. The hope of Israel was fundamentally *soteriological* (from the Greek *soter,* savior). It rested on God's clear promises to the patriarchs and on His evident fulfillment of those promises in the course of history, particularly in the Exodus, which remained always *the* great saving act of Yahweh and the pledge of continued and ultimate "salvation." That salvation consisted in a final, definitive intervention of Yahweh in history by which He would establish His kingdom in Israel and all nations would turn to it for leadership. Thus their hope took on an *eschatological* coloring, in that it looked to an indefinite end-time (from the Greek *eschaton,* last, final). Gradually this kingdom came to be seen as centered in the Davidic dynasty; the *messianic* hope of Israel became, then, characteristically dynastic or royal. But of course a dynasty needs a representative, a king, and so their hopes inevitably centered on an ideal ruler of the line of David. This personal messianism marked the term of their thinking on the subject, although, as a matter of fact, it was the kingdom rather than the king which was the primary object of their hope. It is interesting to note that the hope which had sustained them from the beginning became "messianic" only after the institution of the monarchy, in all likelihood because at that time the Davidic dynasty became the concrete expression, the vehicle of the covenant relationship on which that hope was ultimately based.

The Magna Carta of royal or dynastic messianism is the oracle of Nathan in 2 Sam. (Kings) 7:8-16:

> Thus speaks Yahweh of hosts:
> It was I who took you from the folds
> > from following the sheep,
> > > to be prince over my people Israel.
> I was with you wherever you went,
> > cutting your enemies down before you,
> And I will make your name great,
> > like that of the great ones of the earth. . . .
> Yahweh will make you great
> > Yahweh will make a house of you.
> When your days are completed,
> > and you sleep with your fathers,
> I will raise up descendants after you,
> > the offspring of your body
> > and I will make firm his kingship.
> I will be a father to him,
> > and he a son to me;
> If he acts wickedly I will chastise him
> > with the rod men use,
> > with blows the sons of men give.
> But my covenant-love shall not be taken from him,
> > as I took it from his predecessor:
> Your house and your kingship shall endure forever before me,
> > your throne is set firm forever.

The perpetuity of the Davidic dynasty is thus assured by Yahweh, and the father-son covenant relationship is realized in the relationship between Yahweh and the king. This same idea is expressed at greater length in Psalm 88 (89). Especially significant is the threat of punishment against any representative of the line who may prove unworthy of his position. But the line will continue forever. And this was precisely the way things worked out throughout the history of the monarchy; it was also the teaching of the prophets. For other expressions of this dynastic messianism, see Psalms 2; 44 (45); 71 (72); 109 (110).

The prophets developed this idea magnificently and not the least of their contributions was a marked spiritualization of the concept. Not having any clear notion of the nature of the messianic kingdom, they described it usually in colors which contrasted sharply with the unhappy conditions of their own days. Thus, when social injustice was rampant, they pictured an era in which justice would assure everyone a fair share of blessings, as in Mich. 4:4:

> Every man shall sit under his own vine
> or under his own fig tree, undisturbed;
> For the mouth of the LORD of hosts has spoken.

In times of unrest and war they depicted an era of universal peace, as in the same passage from Micheas:

> In days to come
> the mount of the LORD's house
> Shall be established higher than the mountains;
> it shall rise above the hills
> And peoples shall stream to it:
> many nations shall stream to it, and say,
> "Come, let us climb the mount of the LORD,
> to the house of the God of Jacob,
> That he may instruct us in his ways,
> that we may walk in his paths."
> For from Sion shall go forth instruction,
> and the word of the LORD from Jerusalem.
> He shall judge between many peoples
> and impose terms on strong and distant nations;
> They shall beat their swords into plowshares,
> and their spears into pruning hooks;
> One nation shall not raise the sword against another,
> nor shall they train for war again (4:1-3).

Perhaps the earliest, and surely one of the most beautiful expressions of dynastic messianism in the writings of the prophets is the following:

> But you, Bethlehem-Ephratha,
>   too small to be among the clans of Juda,
> From you shall come forth for me
>   one who is to be ruler in Israel;
> Whose origin is from of old,
>   from ancient times.
> (Therefore the Lord will give them up, until the time
>   when she who is to give birth has borne,
> And the rest of his brethren shall return
>   to the children of Israel.)
> He shall stand firm and shepherd his flock
>   by the strength of the LORD,
>   in the majestic name of the LORD, his God;
> And they shall remain, for now his greatness
>   shall reach to the ends of the earth;
>   he shall be peace (Mich. 5:1-4).

Bethlehem here stands not so much for a geographical indication as for a figure of the Davidic dynasty; it was from here that David came. Note how the prophet sedulously avoids the word "king"; the kings of the dynasty had by that time dragged this title in the mud. He prefers "ruler" or "shepherd." The last line is a perfect expression of the spiritual nature of the Messiah and his kingdom. "Peace" meant much more to the Hebrews than the mere absence of conflict. It was a very positive concept, rich in connotations, and in this context is practically equivalent to "salvation," with all the blessings implied in that term.

"She who is to give birth" suggests the famous prophecy of Micheas' great contemporary, Isaias. When King Achaz, a most unworthy representative of the Davidic dynasty, was preparing Jerusalem's defenses at the time of the Syro-Ephraimitic War, the prophet went to persuade him not to call on the Assyrians for help. With him he took his son Shear-yashub (A Remnant Shall Return — a very significant messianic name, especially under the circumstances, for the course of action being taken by the king would eventually leave only a Remnant in the land). He assured the king that their only hope lay in Yahweh and that he should forget this insane alliance. Such talk was nonsense to a man like Achaz. Isaias even offered to perform a miracle in support of the reliability of his advice. The king met this offer with sneering sarcasm.

Well, Achaz would get a sign from heaven whether he wanted one or not. The one that had been offered him in the first place would have been completely reassuring; the one he actually received was a strange admixture of threat and promise:

> Then he said: Listen, O house of David! Is it not enough for you to weary men, must you also weary my God? Therefore the Lord himself will give you this sign: the virgin shall be with child, and bear a son, and shall name him Emmanuel. He shall be living on curds and honey by the time he learns to reject the bad and choose the good. For before the child learns to reject the bad and choose the good, the land of those two kings whom you dread shall be deserted.
>
> The LORD shall bring upon you and your people and your father's house days worse than any since Ephraim seceded from Juda (7:14-17).

The name of the mysterious child, Emmanuel, means "God with us," and contains a promise of divine intervention in favor of the Chosen People. But Achaz will not profit by this heaven-sent aid. His bullheadedness and lack of faith will bring humiliation and near ruin to the dynasty of which he is the representative. Indeed, things will come to such a pass that the child will spend his infancy in poverty and will have only the crudest foods for his nourishment. Syria and Israel will be brought low, yes, but Juda will have to pay a terrible price for their defeat.

This prophecy strikes the keynote of a development which begins in Is. 7:1 and reaches a glorious climax in chapters 11 and 12. The last chapters suppose a different historical background, but logically they complete the picture of Emmanuel. All Catholic scholars recognize in Emmanuel a figure of the future Messiah. The only question is the manner in which the prophecy is to be understood. Do the words refer directly to the Messiah? Or do they refer immediately to someone soon to be born, like Ezechias, the godly son of Achaz, who would in turn be a type of him who alone would fulfill perfectly the terms of the prophecy, the virgin-born Messiah himself? The latter opinion is gaining more and more favor in Catholic circles; but really, the way in which the prophecy refers to the Messiah is relatively unimportant. The fact that it does point to him is beyond question.

> For a child is born to us, a son is given to us;
>   upon his shoulder dominion rests.
> They name him Wonder-Counselor, God-Hero,
>   Father-Forever, Prince of Peace.
> His dominion is vast
>   and forever peaceful,
> From David's throne, and over his kingdom,
>   which he confirms and sustains
> By judgment and justice,
>   both now and forever,
> The zeal of the LORD of hosts will do this! (Is. 9:5-6).

This is an excellent example of the prophet's taking occasion of an actual historical occurrence to express his hopes for the messianic future. The occasion in this instance was perhaps the birth of Achaz' son, Ezechias. Notice the evident spiritualization of the dynastic concept. There is no mention of fierce conquests in which Israel's enemies are ground into the dust, but rather of a Prince of Peace, whose dominion is peaceful and marked by judgment and justice. See also the truly magnificent development of this idea in 11:1-9.

These few examples from the writings of the prophets illustrate an important stage in the messianic thinking of the Jews. But it was only a stage, and the thinking continued, not always for the better. The development recorded within the sacred pages was, of course, inspired and authentic, but in unofficial, extrabiblical circles, it sometimes took some strange turns. But to finish the biblical development, after the fall of the house of David and the beginning of the Exile, the dynastic idea is rarely encountered. The Suffering Servant of Second Isaias and the Son of Man of Daniel are strong messianic types, but only because the Messiah, when He came, revealed their relevance.

The Jews do not seem to have given them any consistent messianic interpretation. And this is understandable: how reconcile the picture of a Suffering Servant with that of a glorious King?

As the time of His coming drew nearer, the messianic hopes of the people grew more and more confused, thanks in large part to the popularity of extrabiblical writings on the subject, particularly those of the apocalyptic sort. Some of the latter were very beautiful and continued in the line of authentic prophetic teaching. Others, however, were wildly nationalistic and fired the popular imagination. It is no simple matter, then, to say just what sort of Messiah Jesus' contemporaries were expecting, since there were so many different currents of thought in the air.

. A good example is the messianic doctrine of the sectaries of Qumran, from whose caves have come the Dead Sea Scrolls. They apparently looked forward to the coming of two Messiahs, one from the line of David (a king) and another from the line of Sadoc (a high priest). And in the scrolls, as in some of the other literature of this period, the Aaronic or priestly Messiah takes precedence over the royal.

It remained for Jesus to fulfill in His person all the authentic hopes of His people. But the fulfillment was not a literal one; it could not be. For the reality completely transcended the hopes which led to it. There is only an analogous relationship between the kingship of David and that of Jesus, between even an ideal Davidic kingdom and the Kingdom of Heaven, between the virgin of Isaias 7:14 and the Virgin Mother of God. The Jews may have dreamed of an extraordinary intervention of Yahweh in human history; they could never have dreamed that He would actually come into the world in the person of His Son. But He did, and all the inspired hopes of the prophets were fulfilled in a transcendent manner such as only an all-wise and all-loving God could have devised.

Part II

THE NEW TESTAMENT

XI

THE BIRTH OF THE MESSIAH

The expectations of the Chosen People, even the inspired hopes of their prophets, were no match for the love of God. No one of them would have, could have, dreamed that He would send His own Son to rescue them from their sorry plight. Indeed, they had not the slightest idea that He had a Son to send, for the necessary emphasis of the Old Testament on monotheism had kept the mystery of the Trinity just that: a complete mystery. But now the time had come for God to reveal both His true nature and the amazing depths of His love.

One last prophet was to appear on the scene, the immediate herald of the Messiah: John the Baptist. His father, a priest from the hill-country of Juda, was in Jerusalem taking his turn in the carrying out of the temple liturgy. The priests had been divided into twenty-four groups or classes and each class put in a week's service in rotation. On this particular day Zachary was assigned the coveted task of offering incense before the Holy of Holies. As he stood there all alone, intent on his work, an angel announced to him that his prayer had been heard and that his wife Elizabeth would bear him a son whom they were to call John. He could hardly believe his ears; in fact for a moment he did not believe them, for both he and Elizabeth were quite old and had just about given up hope of ever having a child. The angel told him that because of his unbelief he would be unable to speak until the promise was actually fulfilled.

Back home in their little hill-town once more, Elizabeth soon became pregnant, and when she was in her sixth month, the angel announced another and infinitely more momentous birth. He was sent to an obscure village in Galilee called Nazareth. How strange God's ways are! The announcement of the prophet's birth was made to a priest in the temple in Jerusalem. The announcement of the Messiah's birth was made to a teen-age girl in a simple little house in a provincial hamlet. The girl's name was Mary and she was engaged to a carpenter named Joseph. Carpenter though he may have been, still he could trace his ancestry back to the great king David. The royal line had been reduced to impotence after the fall of Jerusalem back in 587, but like many of the nonruling royal families in Europe today it continued its existence.

The angel's greeting was enough to startle anyone, let alone a simple young girl, into utter amazement. "Hail, full of grace, the Lord is with thee. Blessed art thou among women" (Luke 1:28). Is it any wonder that for some moments she was stunned into bewildered silence, puzzling over the possible implications of the words she had heard? For she was lowly not only in social status; her humility was deep and genuine. The angel had to break the embarrassed silence. "Do not be afraid, Mary, for thou hast found grace with God. And behold thou shalt conceive in thy womb, and shalt bring forth a son; and thou shalt call his name Jesus. He shall be great and shall be called the Son of the Most High, and the Lord God will give him the throne of David his father, and he shall be king over the house of Jacob forever; and of his kingdom there shall be no end" (Luke 1:30-33).

These words, falling on the ears of a Jewish girl steeped in the sacred traditions of her people, could have only one meaning: she was to be the mother of the Messiah. Her son would be also the Son of the Most High. Whether Mary understood all the implications of this title at the moment can be questioned, but certainly it indicated that her son would enjoy a very special relationship to God. And he would be a king, the long-awaited successor of the ideal king David — not just another king, but one who would rule forever over an eternal kingdom. St. Luke, who records this singular encounter between heaven and earth, does not even attempt to describe the tumult raging in Mary's virginal breast. He simply reports her incredibly calm answer: "How shall this be done, for I know not man?"

These words, for all their simplicity, have raised all sorts of questions. Their obvious meaning is: "How can I have a son in view of the fact that I have no intention of performing the marital act?" ("To know" in this context meant, in Hebrew idiom, to have intercourse.) If such was her intention, why was she engaged to be married? And while vows of virginity are not uncommon nowadays, have we any right to postulate such a vow in an age and culture wherein virginity was not highly regarded and motherhood was considered the most sublime fulfillment of woman's existence? Even if we grant this possibility, what of Joseph? Are we to presume that he had taken a similar vow? Well, really, there need be no question of a vow, which is a rather technical procedure. Mary may simply have decided to remain a virgin and Joseph may have been just the type of gentleman to respect her wishes. But would not have such an arrangement been highly unusual? Yes, it would have been unusual, but not extraordinarily so, to judge from what the Dead Sea Scrolls have told us about marital arrangements current in some contemporary circles. And even if we grant that it was most unusual, was not the Incarnation unusual, to say the least? Was not the Immaculate Conception unusual, that unique privilege by which God prepared Mary to be the mother of His sinless Son? The Son of God was to become man — an event so extraordinary that we couldn't even imagine it if it hadn't actually happened! What right have we to demand that God bring this event to pass in an "ordinary" way, meaning, of course, a way which respects human procedures? Had He fulfilled these demands, there would have been no Incarnation, no Redemption.

The traditional view of Mary's statement, then, remains the best from all points of view. Gabriel seems to have understood it in that way, for he went on to assure her that her child would not be conceived in the ordinary way: "The Holy Spirit shall come upon thee and the power of the Most High shall overshadow thee; and therefore the Holy One to be born shall be called the Son of God" (Luke 1:35). His words were most significant to one familiar with the Old Testament scriptures. Therein the glory of God was described as "overshadowing" the Tabernacle. Mary, then, will be the Tabernacle of the Most High, the Ark of the (New) Covenant. Rich indeed are the implications of Gabriel's answer.

, He goes on to give Mary a positive sign of the truth of all he has told her: "And behold Elizabeth, thy kinswoman, also has conceived a son in her old age, and she who was called barren is now in her sixth month; for nothing shall be impossible with God" (Luke 1:36-37). But she has asked for no such guarantee; with quiet faith she accepts the divine plan, not really knowing what lies in store for her but trusting God to bring all things to a happy conclusion: "Behold the handmaid of the Lord; be it done unto me according to thy word" (Luke 1:38). With her humble consent, the Son of God takes up residence in her virginal womb. The prophecy of Isaias is on its way to undreamed of fulfillment: "The virgin shall be with child, and bear a son, and shall call him Emmanuel" (7:14). St. Matthew, who quotes this prophecy in connection with Jesus' birth, unfolds its full implications by translating Emmanuel for his readers: "God with us" (1:22-23).

Having heard of Elizabeth's unexpected condition, Mary set out to visit her. She had learned of the situation from a heavenly messenger, and now the Holy Spirit enlightened the older woman's mind to recognize Mary for what she was. "And it came to pass, that when Elizabeth heard the salutation of Mary, the infant leaped in her womb. And Elizabeth was filled with the Holy Ghost, and she cried out with a loud voice, and said: Blessed art thou among women, and blessed is the fruit of thy womb! And whence is this to me, that the mother of my Lord should come to me? For behold as soon as the voice of thy salutation sounded in my ears, the infant in my womb leaped for joy. And blessed is she who has believed that those things shall be accomplished that were spoken to her by the Lord" (Luke 1:41-45). Mary, in an ecstasy of joy and exaltation, replied with the loveliest of canticles, the Magnificat.

Nourished on the scriptures, she sang of her own marvelous exaltation in phrases borrowed from the inspired words of the sacred pages she knew so well (Luke 1:46-55).

She stayed with Elizabeth until just before or just after the birth of John; it is difficult to tell precisely when she left. But at any rate, the new baby now occupies the limelight, as new babies usually do. His birth was the occasion of more than ordinary rejoicing in view of all the circumstances. Among other things, Elizabeth insisted that he be called John — against all the rules; as the first-born, he should have been given his grandfather's name. But Zachary backed up his wife's choice by writing on a tablet: "John is his name." The angel's prophecy was fulfilled and Zachary had followed his instructions in naming the child. On the spot he recovered his power of speech and gave expression to all his pent up emotions in the vigorous Benedictus, wherein he proclaimed that his son had been chosen to act as herald for the Messiah — indeed, for the Lord (Luke 1:68-79).

Some time after Mary returned to Nazareth her condition became apparent to Joseph, and he was understandably puzzled. Knowing nothing of the supernatural cause of her pregnancy, he could draw only one conclusion. But a thousand and one doubts tormented him. The Mary he knew and loved, the Mary who was so eager to preserve her integrity even within the married state — she couldn't possibly have been guilty of deliberate infidelity. Perhaps, then, someone had done violence to her during her visit down south. But her blissful serenity gave the lie to this conjecture. Espousals were considered legally as binding as marriage, and infidelity during that period amounted to adultery in the eyes of the law. Joseph, then, had the right to give her a bill of divorce with all the attendant unsavory publicity. But "being a just man" (Matt. 1:19), that is, a fair and considerate man, he decided rather to find a way of breaking the engagement quietly, without fanfare. Hurt and puzzled though he was, he could still not believe Mary guilty of conduct as base as her condition seemed to indicate. He would not embarrass her.

Why didn't he ask Mary herself? Perhaps because he was the thoughtful type who likes to figure things out for himself, to be sure of his own mind before speaking. Eventually he would have to bring up the subject, of course, but before he had a chance, the Lord appeared to him in a dream and explained what had happened. Thus reassured he took Mary into his own house, a gesture which marked the transition from engagement to marriage.

The story of Jesus' birth is so well known as to need no retelling here. Who has not heard of the census which sent Joseph to his ancestral city of Bethlehem to register, of the crowded conditions which forced him and Mary to seek shelter in a hillside cave, of Mary's delivery there, of the manger, the shepherds, the Magi, the flight into Egypt? Far less generally shared, however, is an appreciation of the gospel accounts of these events. Each of them is, in its own way, a theology of the Incarnation. It is so easy to be beguiled by the charm of the narrative into missing the profundity of its message. Why are the Nativity accounts of Luke and Matthew so different? Because each of them took a special view of the Christ-event and selected and presented the available data with an eye to projecting that view.

Luke, with his usual artistry, paints a diptych with John in one panel and Jesus in the other. The parallels are striking: both births announced by an angel, a reaction of incredulity in one case and a humble request for information in the other; both births described in some detail; two canticles: Mary's Magnificat and Zachary's Benedictus, a name imposed by heaven on each child. But when the pictures are compared, John's — marvelous though it is — pales into insignificance alongside that of Jesus. Mary, too, is described with many subtle allusions to the Old Testament scriptures which leave no doubt in the reader's mind that she is indeed the virgin mother of God, the Ark of the Covenant, resting place of the Most

High, who "overshadows" her with His creative power. Luke's gospel is the gospel of the poor: it is to lowly shepherds that the angels announce peace and joy; it is these humble souls who are privileged to render first homage to the incarnate God. Jerusalem is the focal point of Luke's gospel. It was there that the central events of man's redemption took place, the Passion and Resurrection and Ascension. All through his gospel there is a dramatic movement towards the Holy City. The opening scene is the apparition to Zachary in the temple and the very last verses are: "They worshipped him, and returned to Jerusalem with great joy. And they were continually in the temple, praising and blessing God" (24:52-53). The infancy account likewise reaches its dramatic climax in the temple, on the occasion of the Presentation. Mary was required by law to present herself for ritual purification forty days after giving birth to Jesus. There the old man Simeon met her, took her child in his arms, and gave voice to a canticle which expressed the surpassing dignity of her Son and the real scope of His work:

"Now thou dost dismiss thy servant, O Lord,
    according to thy word, in peace;
Because my eyes have seen thy salvation,
    which thou has prepared before the face of all peoples:
A light of revelation to the Gentiles,
    and a glory for thy people Israel" (Luke 2:29-32).

Matthew has other preoccupations. He is intent on showing that Jesus is indeed the Messiah promised by the prophets and proves his point with far less subtlety than Luke. Not content with describing events in terms suggestive of pertinent Old Testament passages, he quotes those passages directly and interprets the events of the infancy in their light. But he too can be subtle in his own way. One of his central themes is the rejection of the Messiah by the Jews and His acceptance by the Gentiles. Is not this the message of the duplicity of Herod and the adoration of the Magi? For him, too, Jesus is the new Moses, the supreme Lawgiver of the New Covenant, and very adroitly he weaves into the Magi story phrases borrowed from the Moses story in the Old Testament. The Exodus theme also figures prominently in his account. Jesus is the new Israel exiled in Egypt but returning to the Promised Land to flourish eventually as the the Church, the eternal Christ, Head and members. To this end he pointedly applies Osee 11:1 to Jesus' return to Palestine: "Out of Egypt I have called my son," words which in their original context refer to the return of Israel from bondage.

And finally there is the prologue to St. John's gospel, a sublime and forthright theology of the Incarnation. The disciple whom Jesus loved, after years of devout meditation on the birth of Jesus, distilled from all the circumstances of that event its sublime essence: "The Word was made flesh, and dwelt among us" (1:14). Who can miss the wonder which breathes through those words? It is a wonder which this same apostle was to express elsewhere in other words: "For God so loved the world that he gave his only-begotten Son, that those who believe in him may not perish, but may have life everlasting" (3:16). "In this has the love of God been shown in our case, that God has sent his only-begotten Son into the world that we may live through him" (1 John 4:9).

XII

THE HIDDEN LIFE OF JESUS

Upon their return from Egypt the Holy Family went back up to Nazareth in Galilee. Herod had died in 4 B.C. and the Romans, of whom he had really been just an astute puppet, had split his kingdom among his sons. Archelaus had run to Rome as soon as was decent after the death of his father and began to pull strings, of which he had several, with a view to being named king in Herod's place. But his subjects were just as nimble as he was. They sent a delegation of prominent citizens to beg Caesar Augustus to abolish the kingship in Judea and attach Palestine to the Roman province of Syria. One can judge from this desperate move how completely disgusted they were with the Herodian family. They would rather see their beloved country reduced to the humble status of a minor satellite than suffer a continuance of the heavy-handed Herodian hegemony.

As a result of their pleas, Augustus reduced Archelaus' rank to that of ethnarch but granted him the bulk of his father's territory: Judea, Samaria, and Idumea. The glittering capital, Jerusalem, was his to enjoy, and although he could not glory in the title of king, he could console himself with all the trappings of royalty. His brother Herod Philip II became tetrarch of the northeastern districts of Iturea and Trachonitis; Herod Antipas got Galilee and Perea. It was under the direct rule of the latter, consequently, that Jesus grew up.

His boyhood is passed over by the Evangelists in almost unbroken silence. After describing the presentation in the temple, St. Luke, who does not record the flight into Egypt, states quite simply: "And when they had fulfilled all things as prescribed in the Law of the Lord, they returned into Galilee, to their own town of Nazareth. And the child grew and became strong. He was full of wisdom and the grace of God was upon him" (2:39-40). He will break the silence only to tell of the trip to Jerusalem when Jesus was twelve years old.

We can, then, only surmise what His boyhood was like, but our conjectures are not mere wild guesses. After all, we do know a great deal about what life was like in a little Galilean town in the first century of our era. And since the Holy Family lived that life in quite ordinary fashion, it is not difficult to fit them into the picture. Nazareth itself nestled in the soft hills of Galilee. A poor little village, indeed an object of contempt for Jesus' contemporaries, it made up for its poverty by the richness of its natural setting. Joseph's home consisted, in all likelihood, of one room, mostly underground, as it was the fashion to hollow houses out of the soft limestone of the hills. (In this event, the cave outside of Bethlehem had been rather like home, at least after it had been cleaned up a bit.) There were no "modern conveniences"; water for washing and cooking came from the village well, still in existence, where Mary went to fetch it in an earthenware jar perched securely atop her strong young head. She did her laundry at the community washtub or perhaps at a nearby stream, literally beating the dirt out of the soiled clothes with a stick while exchanging local news with her neighbors.

In such a simple setting material needs were few, and Joseph was able to keep his family as comfortable as the next. Their diet was quite uncomplicated: bread, a few vegetables, milk, very occasionally some meat — usually lamb — or fish. But Jesus thrived on it, and St. Luke rather pointedly informs us that "the child grew and became strong." In the mild climate of Galilee He most likely spent most of His time out of doors, romping with His playmates and turning brown as a berry from exposure to the sun. He was at home in the fields and hills, feasted His eyes on the wildflowers dotting the rolling landscape, listened to the birds chirping gaily in olive and cypress trees, watched them frolicking in the bougainvillea vines. One needs only recall His later parables to realize what a deep impression all these sights and sounds made on His sensitive young soul. But He learned not only from nature. He would have attended school at the local synagogue, there to become versed in the Torah, the Law — His Law! There were no books; only the fortunate few learned to read. The pupils sat around in a circle on the floor and repeated the sacred texts over and over again until they knew them by heart — a system, by the way, which developed the memory of the Semite to an extent that seems almost incredible to us who live in an age of books.

In some such simple, carefree, fashion Jesus passed His boyhood. But when He reached the age of twelve He was considered by the Law no longer a boy. He was a *bar-mitzvah,* a son of the Law, responsible for the observance of its all-en-compassing prescriptions. Among the latter was the duty of making an annual pilgrimage to the temple, if this were at all possible. Accordingly, Joseph and Mary took Him with them for the celebration of the great Passover feast. Imagine what an exciting adventure this must have been for a twelve-year-old boy who had never been outside his little village. The cara-van, the chants of pilgrimage, the gay camaraderie of people on a holiday, thrilling new sights and sounds, new companions, seldom seen cousins of His own age. Unable to suppress His excitement, He flitted from group to group, visiting now with this aunt, this uncle, this cousin. But surely, deep down in His soul, He was aware of the dramatic significance of this pil-grimage. There would come a day when He would go up to the Passover in Jerusalem to celebrate His Last Supper. On the morrow He would be the Paschal Lamb and they would drain every last drop of His blood and pierce His broken heart, and He would offer Himself as Victim for the sins of the world. Significantly, with his fine dramatic sense of the cen-tral place of Jerusalem in the divine plan, Luke alone records this early journey to the Holy City.

After the celebration of the feast the caravan regrouped and started back north. Jesus had been so frequently away from His parents visiting with relatives that they took it for granted He was with some of His cousins enjoying the hubbub of de-parture from the city. But when they stopped to encamp for the night they became uneasy. Flit about as He may have during the day, He always came to have supper with His parents and to sleep in the warm security of their nearness. But tonight He failed to appear. We can imagine Mary getting more and more worried as she went about preparing the evening meal and finally sending Joseph off to look for Him. We can imagine, too, her dismay when Joseph returned alone, a worried frown creasing his strong brown forehead. In near panic they left the caravan and retraced their steps to Jerusalem, making anxious inquiries all along the road and receiving nothing but embarrass-

ing shrugs of the shoulders in reply. At length they were all the
way back to Jerusalem. But where to find a little boy in these
winding alleys, these crowded bazaars? Where to start looking?
The temple was as logical a place as any, and there they came
upon Him.

In the long stately porticoes which lined the immense courtyard, the famous rabbis of the day held their classes. Each of
them would gather his pupils about him and they would squat
cross-legged on the pavement listening and questioning. The
atmosphere was like that of Jesus' little synagogue class back
home, even if on a grander scale, and He felt quite at ease.
He squatted with some other boys on the fringe of one of the
groups and listened with rapt attention. And with that dis-
arming lack of self-consciousness which boys can display in
the most unexpected situations, He interjected a few questions
of His own, questions which were so acute as to cause raised
eyebrows all around.

When Mary espied Him, she concealed her profound relief
by the typically maternal device of gently scolding Him: "Son,
why hast thou done so to us? Behold, thy father and I have
been seeking thee sorrowing." With a poise that belied His
years, He answered quite calmly, "How is it that you sought
me? Did you not know that I must be about my Father's business?" Luke, whose information must have come at least in-
directly from Mary, hastens to add: "And they did not understand the word that he spoke to them" (2:50).

Jesus' answer, in cold print, could sound rather flip. But
the tone of voice in which He uttered it very probably con-
veyed a deeply sympathetic concern. At the same time, it communicated to Mary and Joseph a bit of information about Him
which contributed to their gradual awareness of what His mission involved. They knew at the very least that He was the
Messiah, but they were to learn only gradually just how He
was to carry out in practice His messianic work. His somewhat
cryptic answer on this occasion went straight to Mary's heart,
not to wound, but to be pondered in wondering meditation.

And as if to dispel any possible impression of filial disrespect, Luke continues: "And he went down with them and came to Nazareth, and was subject to them; and his mother kept all these things carefully in her heart. And Jesus advanced in wisdom and age and grace before God and men" (2:51-52).

The whole tenor of the foregoing narrative implies most strongly that Jesus was an only child. Certainly if Mary and Joseph had other children they would have had them by the time He was twelve. And yet there is the annoying question of Jesus' "brothers and sisters," annoying not because it constitutes a problem but simply because it is raised at all. True, we read in Mark 3:31: "And his mother and his brethren came, and standing outside, they sent to him, calling him." And in Mark 6:3: "Is not this the carpenter, the son of Mary, the brother of James, Joseph, Jude, and Simon? And are not also his sisters here with us?" It is rather significant, however, that Jesus is distinguished from His "brothers" and "sisters" as "the son of Mary." The fact is that Hebrew and Aramaic designate by these terms any number of relationships, close or distant, and the Evangelists, although writing in Greek, preserved the Aramaic idiom of Jesus and His contemporaries. In Gen. 14:14 Abraham's nephew Lot is spoken of as his brother, and in Gen. 29:15 Jacob is called the brother of his uncle Laban. Perhaps more pertinent is 1 Par. 23:21-22, where the sons of Cis are referred to as the "brothers" of their cousins, the daughters of Eleazar. The brothers of Jesus of whom we read in the gospels were in all probability his cousins. This has been the constant tradition of the Church, a tradition based on sound reasons of all sorts. The subject has been treated at great length by many authors and there is no need to prolong the discussion here, except to point out one more significant fact. Jesus took great pains to entrust Mary to the care of St. John that last afternoon on Calvary. Would this have been necessary, or even natural, if Mary had other sons and daughters to whom she could turn?

In later years Jesus was known as "the carpenter, the son

of Mary." The latter epithet suggests most strongly that He was at that time the only son of a widow. And since there is not the slightest mention of Joseph during our Lord's public ministry, there is good reason to suppose that he died while Jesus was still a young man. Before his death, however, he did for his foster son what every good Jewish father was expected to do: he taught Him a trade. Even the rabbis, men who devoted themselves to intellectual and moral pursuits, were required to be skilled in some craft or other. The renowned Hillel was a woodcutter and the equally famous Shammai a carpenter. The even more renowned Paul was a tentmaker. Whether it was expected or not, the prudent Joseph would have seen to it that Jesus was able to support His mother should she ever have to depend upon Him alone. And so He who had fashioned the universe, He through whom were made all things that were made, learned to make chests and beds and chairs and poles and yokes. How ironic that He who worked with wood for a living should Himself be nailed to a piece of wood one day to die.

While He worked so calmly in little out-of-the-way Nazareth, the political situation which would form the background for His public ministry was slowly taking shape. In 6 A.D. Augustus deposed Archelaus and appointed a Roman procurator to rule over the territory he had held. The fourth of these procurators, who arrived in 26 A.D., was to play a sinister role in the drama of man's redemption. His name was Pontius Pilate. It was about this same time that Herod Antipas, who still ruled in Galilee, divorced his wife and started living openly with his sister-in-law Herodias. They, too, were to figure in the gospel story.

The Hidden Life of Jesus has often caused men to wonder. Why should God come to earth and then spend about nine-tenths of His earthly career in utter obscurity? Well, if it were only to demonstrate once more that God's ways are not our ways, that would be reason enough. Sometimes men find it difficult to realize that; they would be so much more comfortable if He were more like them. But the purpose of the Incarnation was not to lower God to the level of the human. It was rather to raise men to the level of the divine. The Hidden Life was an essential part of this process. It taught us the divine value of humility, obedience, honest manual labor, family life irradiated by charity — virtues not generally held in high esteem by a sophisticated world, but virtues which would be demanded by those who would give their allegiance to Him whose kingdom is not of this world.

XIII

JESUS BEGINS HIS PUBLIC LIFE

"Now in the fifteenth year of the reign of Tiberius Caesar, when Pontius Pilate was procurator of Judea, and Herod tetrarch of Galilee, and Philip his brother tetrarch of the district of Iturea and Trachonitis, and Lysanias tetrarch of Abilina, during the high priesthood of Annas and Caiphas, the word of God came to John, the son of Zachary, in the desert. And he went into all the region about the Jordan, preaching a baptism of penance for the forgiveness of sins . . . John addressed them saying to all, 'I indeed baptize you with water. But one mightier than I is coming, the strap of whose sandals I am not worthy to loose. He will baptize you with the Holy Spirit and with fire' " (Luke 3:1-3, 16).

John the Baptist had spent much of his youth — he was now about thirty — in the desert of Judea. His parents' home was not far from there and he had apparently been attracted by the life of solitary contemplation led by so many of his compatriots. In this forbidding wasteland scarred by gullies and ravines, noble-minded Jews from all walks of life had settled down in cheerless caves to devote themselves to uninterrupted study and prayer. Their motives were, of course, varied. Some were temperamentally drawn to such an existence; others were fed up with the conduct of the religious leaders of the people. Their mode of life was not uniform, either: some lived quite alone, as John seems to have done; others formed little communities. The most famous of the latter was that of Qumran, on the shore of the Dead Sea; it is from their caves that the Dead Sea scrolls came. It is highly probable that John was acquainted with these sectaries, but it is not at all certain that he was one of their number. His teaching is so different from theirs on so many points.

• His sojourn in the desert was, at any rate, not so very unusual. Since his parents were well along in years when he was born, they may well have died before he was far into young manhood. All alone then, he took up the rugged life which suited his temperament so well. And there in the desert the word of the Lord came to him as it had to so many of the prophets in the past. Their task had been to keep alive in the hearts of the people the saving hope which looked to the Messiah, and to induce them to live lives worthy of that coming. John's task was similar but much more significant. They pointed to a distant event, the exact time of which was quite uncertain. He was the herald of the Messiah already in their midst. "Repent, for the kingdom of heaven is at hand" (Matt. 3:2). The long-awaited kingdom was about to be established and if they wished to enter it, they would have to "repent," to change their outlook and conduct radically. Those who accepted his message made a humble avowal of their past sinfulness and, as a sign of their new dispositions, submitted to a ritual washing, a baptism, at John's hands. Such lustrations were quite common in Jewish circles of the day, but they were so typical of John's ministry that he got to be known popularly as "the baptizer," "the Baptist."

One day his cousin Jesus stepped forward, unannounced, from the crowd he had been addressing, and requested baptism. John was as startled as all who have read this passage have ever been. "It is I who ought to be baptized by thee, and dost thou come to me?" But Jesus answered and said to him, "Let it be so now, for so it becomes us to fulfill all justice" (Matt. 3:14-15). When He had been baptized, He saw the Holy Spirit hovering over Him in the form of a dove and heard His Father proclaim, "This is my beloved Son, in whom I am well pleased." It is not usual that all four Evangelists record the same event — John usually goes his own way — but they all describe Jesus' baptism, sensing, no doubt, its profound significance. Jesus had chosen this moment to inaugurate His messianic career of teaching and healing and suffering and dying and rising. It was to be a career marked by humility and humiliation. The sinless Savior who was to die for sinners inaugurated His work by a gesture of humility which associated Him with sinful mankind. At the same time the other two Persons of the Blessed Trinity proclaimed His innocence and put the divine stamp of approval on His work.

There followed almost immediately an event of even greater mystery: the temptation in the desert. After His baptism, Jesus withdrew into that same desert region which John called his home. There, in rapt communion with the Father and the Holy Spirit, He fasted for forty days and forty nights. And afterwards He was hungry, as the gospel tells us — rather pointlessly, it might seem. The remark is not so banal as it appears. Dazzled by the divinity of Jesus, we may forget the reality of His humanity, imagining perhaps that He, being God, could fast such a long time and feel no ill effects. Not at all; He was hungry, and the tempter, who knew nothing of His divinity but suspected His messianic identity, saw an opening. He who had once made the fruit of the tree look suddenly irresistible to Eve was sure that the mere thought of bread would bend the hungry man to his will. Having failed on this tack he tried two others, appealing to his victim's possible pride and lust for power. But in each instance the victim proved to be the victor.

To appreciate the complete relevance of this scene, one must read it in the general context of Salvation History. Jesus had come to undo the work of Satan, whose successful temptation of Eve had plunged mankind into utter misery. The wily seducer could never forget the curse of which he had been the object. He knew that one day a descendant of Eve's would break his power, "crush his head." Jesus gave every sign of being just that descendant, and now that He had so successfully upset him in this first skirmish, he knew that he was in for a real battle. St. Luke tells us that after his failure to overcome Jesus, he departed from him "for a while" (4:13).

. This event, coming as it did at the outset of our Lord's public life, was a most significant preview of the nature of His messianic mission. He had come to destroy the power of Satan, and all throughout His ministry He drove the demon from possessed souls, achieving victory after victory in anticipation of the supreme conquest of Calvary. There, on the throne of the cross, He would shatter the kingdom of darkness and establish the Kingdom of God on earth. But He would do it in His own way, not in the dazzling worldly fashion which figured so prominently in current messianic expectations. In refusing to work a miracle for His own benefit, in rejecting the suggestion that He descend dramatically from the pinnacle of the temple, in spurning the offer of all the kingdoms of the world, He set the tone for His whole mission. It was to be one of humility, unselfish sacrifice, poverty, and suffering — but it would be supremely victorious. He would establish His kingdom on His own terms, not the world's.

The parallel between Jesus' forty days in the desert and the Exodus is quite striking, too, and establishes a continuity between God's great saving act of old and the incomparably greater act of universal redemption He was to accomplish in the blood of the true Paschal Lamb. Jesus, by "passing over" from death to life, was to lead all men in an exodus from bondage to freedom, from sin to grace and glory. Having symbolically passed through the Red Sea (the waters of the Jordan), He spent forty days in the desert, just as the Israelites had spent forty years on the way to the Promised Land. Their forty years had been precisely a time of testing, of temptation; His forty days culminated in a triple temptation. But where they had often fallen, He was consistently victorious. The suggestion that He turn stones into bread is strongly suggestive of the miraculous manna which had sustained the Israelites. Even the scriptural quotations with which He repelled the three temptations are taken from the account of the Exodus in Deuteronomy. Subtle though the points of contact may be, they are too numerous to have been purely fortuitous. They express a theme dear to the Evangelists, particularly St. Matthew, that of Jesus as the new Moses, the new Israel, conducting a new and perfect Exodus, of which the ancient one was but a pale foreshadowing.

The same theme, particularly in its Passover aspect, figures in the first call of the disciples. When Jesus came down from the mountain to the Jordan valley, John the Baptist was still preaching to all who would listen. Among his hearers were two Galileans who had become quite attached to him: John and Andrew. When Jesus passed nearby, the Baptist pointed to Him and said, "Behold the lamb of God!" The paschal and messianic overtones of the epithet were inescapable, and John and Andrew, fascinated, went to meet Him. Not knowing quite how to approach Him, they simply tagged along behind Him with an eagerness tempered by embarrassment. Then Jesus turned and asked them, with a gentleness which heartened them, "What is it you seek?" Caught off guard, and not really sure just what it was they were seeking, they could think of nothing better by way of answer than "Rabbi, where do you live?" They were rewarded with an invitation which changed their destinies: "Come and see." It was about four in the afternoon, as St. John himself recalls, and they spent the whole evening with Him.

We do not know what they talked about during that first meeting, but there can be no doubt that Jesus impressed them profoundly. For Andrew went running to his brother Simon with the breathless announcement: "We have found the Messiah!" Simon simply had to come and meet Him right away. It was a momentous, even if momentarily mysterious, meeting. Jesus looked at the newcomer and said, "Thou art Simon, the son of

John; Thou shalt be called Cephas." Peter must have been quite puzzled at his new name; it was only much later that Jesus explained why He had designated him as the "Rock." But the significance of the actual change of name could hardly escape him. For among the Semites a name was a sacred thing. It was not merely an identifying label; it was considered in some way as embodying the person himself. Thus, when we pray, "Hallowed be thy name," we mean, "may You be sanctified, glorified." The change of one person's name by another was a very meaningful gesture. Among Semitic peoples, one of the first acts of a victorious king was to change the name of his vanquished rival, thus indicating that the latter was now in his complete power. In pagan nations with their many gods, there was a strong belief that knowing the personal name of a god gave one a certain measure of power over him. And in the sacred history of the Jews themselves there were instances of God's having changed the names of individuals whom He had selected to play prominent roles in that history. Thus Abram, the progenitor of the Chosen People, had become Abraham. Jacob, father of the twelve men who would in turn beget the twelve tribes, became Israel in the midst of a mystical encounter with his God. And so while Peter may have been bewildered at the precise implications of his new name, he sensed that this meeting with his young fellow Galilean was a fateful one. And so it was.

One more disciple was to be added to the little band before they returned to their native Galilee. The next day Jesus met a fellow townsman of Andrew and Peter, Philip of Bethsaida. If Jesus' personal magnetism is evident in the response of the first three disciples, it is even more evident here. He said to the new recruit simply, "Follow me." We are not told what Philip's immediate reaction was, but we may surmise it from the sequel. Philip found Nathanael (also called Bartholomew) and informed him, certainly in great excitement, "We have found him of whom Moses in the Law and the Prophets wrote, Jesus the son of Joseph of Nazareth." Nathanael's first reaction was a very bored, "Can anything good come out of Nazareth?" Undaunted, Philip insisted, "Come and see." And he came and saw and was conquered.

It was three days later that Jesus first appeared at a public gathering with His disciples. A young couple was being married in Cana, just about five miles from Nazareth. They were apparently friends of Mary, for she was there when Jesus arrived. He had been invited, too, and was asked to bring along whatever friends He wished. The Jewish wedding celebration was quite an affair, lasting at least three days and sometimes going on for a week. This put quite a strain on the family budget, but everyone chipped in and preparations went on for weeks in advance. The couple in the gospel story were evidently doing things in grand style; they even had a chief steward or caterer.

The festivities were in high gear when Mary approached Jesus and whispered to Him that they had run out of wine — and what could be more embarrassing on an occasion when wine was of the essence? In a reply which has been translated in many different ways, Jesus intimated that there was nothing they could do about it. But Mary, with that beautiful intuition which God gives to all mothers, and with an even more wonderful intuition enjoyed only by the mother of God, said to the waiters, "Do whatever he tells you." Now, even at a marriage feast, the Jews were careful to perform all the ritual washings prescribed by the Law, and for this purpose there were six large stone water-jars in the room — or perhaps in the flower-decked yard. At Jesus' request the waiters filled them to the brim with sparkling well water and brought them to the chief steward, who was most likely wringing his hands in consternation at the disastrous turn of events. His reputation would be ruined! Puzzled but willing to try anything, he sampled the contents of one of the jars, and his eyes opened wide in delight and wonder. But this was against all the rules of the trade! He called the groom and demanded an explanation. "How come? Don't you know that you should have served the vintage wine first and saved the ordinary stuff for later, when the guests

couldn't care less?" First the bonded stuff, then the blends —
that was his rule of thumb. But the poor groom was as much
at sea as he was. He had no idea where this superb wine had
come from. The waiters knew, though, and it didn't take them
long to spread the word. As a result, St. John informs us, Jesus'
disciples believed in Him. They had more than suspected His
messianic identity after speaking with Him. Now they were sure.
Now they believed.

Readers of this account are often disturbed by the seeming
discourtesy in Jesus' reply to Mary when she informed Him
of the situation. They are particularly dismayed by His addressing her, with seeming coldness, as "Woman." But in the language
which Jesus spoke, this was actually a term of highest respect.
He was to address her thus at the tenderest moment of their
lives, just before He breathed His last. Looking at St. John
standing with her at the foot of the cross, He said to her,
"Woman, behold thy son." And St. John, with his fine sense
of the symbolic, may have seen even deeper into the significance
of this address. For while it was most courteous, it was not the
usual way of speaking to one's mother. Significantly, it is John
again who, in his Apocalypse (12:1-6), gives us a symbolic
description which can be applied to Mary and the Church,
a fusion popular among early Church writers. The central
figure of the symbol is "the woman." May it not be that John
was thinking of the "woman" of Gen. 3:15, the woman between
whom and Satan God placed implacable enmity, the woman
whose seed would crush the Serpent's head? It is not at all
improbable.

Speaking of John's fine sense of the symbolic, scholars are
growing increasingly aware of the symbolism of his gospel,
particularly its sacramental symbolism. The connection of the
Cana incident with Matrimony is obvious, but there are strong
Eucharistic connotations in the event, too, specifically in the
transformation of water into wine. These connotations become
even stronger when we recall John's account of the blood and
water which trickled from the pierced side of Jesus on the

cross. In this latter connection, two phrases in the Cana narrative catch our attention. One is Jesus' mysterious remark to Mary, "My hour is not yet come." In John's gospel Jesus' hour is consistently the hour of His crucifixion, but the crucifixion is, again in the Johannine perspective, His moment of supreme glory. This miracle, then, is an anticipation of that hard-won glory, and John remarks in concluding his narrative: "This first of his signs Jesus worked at Cana of Galilee; and *he manifested his glory,* and his disciples believed in him" (2:11). Subtle? Perhaps. But is not symbolism of its nature subtle? And John was a master symbolist.

· XIV

JESUS TEACHES THE KINGDOM OF GOD

The Son of God had come to crush the head of the Serpent, to restore men to their supernatural dignity as sons of God, to make it possible for them to gain entrance into that Kingdom which He had prepared for them from all eternity. Divine ingenuity could have devised any number of ways to achieve this end. What the method actually was we know, for it was the method of Jesus. Men were to find their salvation within the framework of an earthly kingdom, the temporal counterpart of and preparation for the eternal Kingdom. Within this kingdom men would share, as much as humanly possible, in the divine life which would be their bliss for all eternity. Jesus would die to abolish the old curse of alienation from the Father, and the graces He would win on the cross would be available to all those who believed in Him and abided by the requirements demanded of those who would be members of His life-giving kingdom. But first He must establish the kingdom and prepare the minds and hearts of men to accept it.

So different was this kingdom from those of earth, so different, specifically, from the glittering messianic kingdom expected by the majority of His compatriots, that the minds and hearts of men needed a great deal of preparation. Jesus knew those minds and hearts as only their Creator could. Divine pedagogue, He appealed to them in the simple, clear, picturesque language of the Galilean peasant, language marked by bold imagery, gentle balance, arresting paradox. His words have become so commonplace to us who have heard them over and over again in a variety of contexts from our childhood that it is difficult for us to appreciate their literally revolutionary character. Now to preach a revolutionary doctrine and not precipitate an abortive revolution is no mean accomplishment. Jesus did, in fact, want to effect a revolution, but on His own terms — the kind effected by a bit of yeast in a batch of dough or by a tiny mustard seed quietly fructifying in the warm earth.

All of the Evangelists have given us samples of His teaching, but in this area St. Matthew is most instructive. At the heart of his gospel are five large synthetic sermons on various aspects of the kingdom. They are synthetic because in all likelihood they were not delivered exactly in the form in which he records them. He gathered together significant utterances of the Master and arranged them topically. But thanks to this method we can follow Jesus' instructions on any number of vital points and get a clear picture of His mind and His technique.

One of the most illustrative, and surely the best known, of these great discourses is the Sermon on the Mount. Within this grand synthesis we find a broad statement of the fundamental requirements, individual and social, of membership in the kingdom. We find, too, a clear statement of the essentially spiritual nature of the kingdom, of its superiority over that of the old dispensation. Here on the Mount of the Beatitudes the new Moses proclaims the New Law and, with supreme authority, promulgates it as a perfection of the Old. Jesus insists that He has come not to destroy the divinely sanctioned Law which has guided the Chosen People to this focal point of human history, but rather to perfect it. The whole sermon illustrates how the New Law will perfect the Old, gives instance after instance of its transcendent superiority.

The discourse opens with the Eight Beatitudes, so called because each of them begins, in the Latin text, with the word *"Beati,"* blessed, happy. And what a complete reversal of the world's point of view they express! Jesus declares fortunate those whom the world pities or scorns or ridicules: the poor, the humble, the sorrowful, the hungry, the merciful, the pure of heart, the peaceful, the oppressed. And yet, it is such as these that He has come to call to His kingdom. They are God's little ones, objects of His fatherly love and concern, and He has sent His Son to lead them home. They alone will follow Him, under ordinary circumstances, and anyway they make up the vast majority of the human race. Those whose hearts are set on riches and pleasures will feel no need for Him; the proud sophisticates will sneer or smile indulgently at the impractical idealism of His doctrine; those who value comfort and luxury above all else will shudder and turn away in disgust from the ugliness of the Cross; the selfish will refuse to meet the demands of generous love which He will establish as the essential spirit of His Kingdom.

The passport to the Kingdom is faith, a humble acceptance of the teachings and an equally humble obedience to the laws of the King. Thus the "poor in spirit" get top billing in the Beatitudes: the "poor in spirit," the humble souls whose way of life is simple and wholesome and solidly virtuous. Their hearts are quite unattached and ready to accept God's loving call. Jesus does not extol poverty for its own sake; slums are not usually schools of sanctity, and a pauper's heart can be more greedily attached to riches than that of a wealthy men. What Jesus asks is a disposition of soul, an unselfish humility, a child-like willingness to do the will of a loving Father — whatever that will may entail. It is this disposition which is fundamental to all the Beatitudes, which express various personal qualities recommending one for entrance into the Kingdom.

These qualities are by no means so negative as they may first appear. Poverty of spirit is really a very positive attitude of soul, an eagerness to forsake all for the Kingdom. The meek who are called blessed are not the Casper Milquetoast type at all; they are rather those who patiently, even courageously, maintain their stability and equanimity in the face of adversity. In the pursuit and defense of righteousness they may be actually more like lions than lambs. Witness our Lord's expulsion of the money-changers from the temple or His vehement excoriation of the Pharisees. Those who mourn, too, are sturdy characters. Life may wring tears from their eyes, but they endure its painful vicissitudes staunchly, tears or no tears. Those who hunger and thirst after justice are definitely positive personalities; they are eager to see God's will done all along the line, in their own lives and in the world at large. The merciful are nobly sensitive to those less fortunate than themselves; they are not afraid to feel compassion and to express it in a practical way. Purity of heart is not the virtue of a shrinking violet; it is won only by hard discipline. It is not Puritanical sham which pretends to be dismayed and disgusted at sins of the flesh while secretly taking a morbid delight in them. It is a sincere, interior, wholesomeness which enables a person to pursue the good with single-mindedness and clear vision, and the reward promised is a clear vision of the Supreme Good. The peacemakers are not only those who reconcile enemies and patch up quarrels but, more profoundly, those who pursue peace, which in biblical terminology is tantamount to perfection. And as for those who suffer persecution for justice's sake, has the world ever known any greater heroes than the martyrs? Every age has had its share, and ours is far from being an exception.

Having outlined the personal qualities requisite for entrance into the Kingdom, Jesus touches on the social qualities of its members. They are to be the salt of the earth, seasoning society with the lively flavor of Christian virtue. They are to be the light of the world, beacons drawing all men to the truth and eventually to salvation. The rest of the Sermon as constructed by St. Matthew deals with the New Law's superiority over the Old on several points: anger, impurity, marriage, oaths, retaliation, charity, alms, prayer, fasting. One principle stands out in sharp relief as a determining factor of this superiority, the principle of true interior religion as opposed to external and often hypocritical formalism. If the New Law is superior to that of the Old Testament, it surpasses immeasurably the standards governing life among the pagans, and Jesus illustrates this by teaching the correct attitude towards riches and earthly concerns. He then gives positive rules of charity, discretion, and prayer, and criteria for the discernment of spirits.

The Sermon on the Mount is sometimes presented as containing the sum total of Christ's teaching. This is very far from the truth. It is rather an introduction to His teaching; it lays down the broad principles on which the Kingdom will be based and sets the tone for life within the Kingdom. It is only the first of five great discourses drawn up by Matthew, but it is an excellent example of the teaching of the Master, a sermon which has been called the most revolutionary of all human discourses. Could it have been otherwise? It was the charter of a kingdom such as human history had never known, a kingdom not of this world, a kingdom in which the divine and the human met and blended, a kingdom ruled and vitalized by a God-man.

The literary style of the Sermon has often proved disconcerting to unwary readers who forget that they are reading words uttered almost two millenia ago in an Oriental language fashioned by and reflecting a psychology startlingly different from ours. The Jews were not a philosophical people, at least not in the sense that the Greeks were philosophical. They had no sympathy for abstractions as such and preferred the concrete, the dramatic, the picturesque. This is not to say that abstract concepts were utterly foreign to them. They were vitally concerned with such notions as truth and justice and knowledge and loving kindness. But they had a tendency to concretize them, and Jesus, whose human thought patterns were similarly fashioned, communicated the most sublime truths to them in this very realistic manner.

We must, then, appreciate His bold figures, His hyperbole,

His strong antitheses for what they were: very practical vehicles for the expression of profound truths. To take the prescriptions of the Sermon with strict literalness would be to transform Christians into a flock of simple, wide-eyed sheep just waiting for the butcher's knife. Thanks be to God, the early Christians, whom we may presume to have understood our Lord aright, never believed that one was obliged by the Gospel to gouge out his right eye, cut off his right hand, turn the other cheek to an assailant, or call back a thief who had stolen a cloak but had forgotten to take the tunic as well. If subsequent ages gave occasional evidence of some excesses in the interpretation of these prescriptions, they did so only sporadically and as the result of a misguided fervor, a lack of judgment. We can gauge the manner in which our Lord's immediate hearers understood Him from the actions and attitudes of the first Christians.

Another method of teaching suited to the Semitic flair for the dramatic was the parable. This was a fictitious but quite credible story used to illustrate a truth of faith or morals. Jesus was a master of this very effective pedagogical device and used it over and over again to inculcate startling ideas without startling His hearers, to impose frightening demands without terrifying them. For the point of a parable is not always immediately clear; it is rather like the apparently lifeless seed which the sower places in the ground. The charm of the story makes reception of the idea easy, but once the seed is planted, it springs to life. The hearer begins to turn the story over in his mind, and the more he thinks of it, the more sharply the underlying idea comes into focus.

For many reasons this method was admirably suited to Jesus' purposes. His teaching, His very Person, was revolutionary in the full sense of the term, and He was revealing Himself to people who were highly volatile, chafing as they were under the constant frictions of foreign domination and breathlessly awaiting a liberator who would lead them out from under. The general era of our Lord's activity saw more than its share of false Messiahs who whipped the crowds into a frenzy, fomented rebellions which were doomed before they were born, and led their followers to bloody disaster. Jesus was having none of this. He would carry off His revolution, yes, but slowly, patiently, ever so subtly, and the subtlety of the parable was made to order.

There was, however, an even more profound reason for this cautiously gradual self-revelation on Jesus' part. That reason was the very nature of the revelation itself. To begin with, it was open to serious misunderstanding, and before Jesus could let the full light of His truth burst upon men's souls, He had to prepare those souls. Old ideas had to be carefully eradicated, new ones deftly insinuated. Before He could openly claim kingship, messiahship, He had to make sure people knew what kind of king He was, what kind of kingdom He had come to establish, and in precisely what sense He was the Messiah.

Or take the notion of His divine Sonship. One doesn't simply walk into a crowd and introduce oneself as the Son of God. If the ideas of a spiritual kingship and of a kingdom not of this world were difficult to put across, what shall we say of the idea of divine Sonship? This was an idea so utterly fantastic, humanly speaking, that it could be fully appreciated, if at all, only in the light of the Resurrection and with the help of divine faith. Jesus' task during His ministry was to furnish evidence of His divinity which would cause wonder without repelling and which would be grasped in its full relevance once the Resurrection had given the key to its profound significance. St. Mark especially underscores the gradual character of Jesus' self-revelation and quite pointedly refers over and over again to the lack of comprehension displayed by the disciples themselves. But it could not have been otherwise; the very nature of the revelation demanded it.

In chapter 13, another of his five great synthetic discourses, Matthew has gathered together a large group of our Lord's parables, all of them dealing with some aspect of the Kingdom. Common to them all is the notion of the Kingdom as a mystery. Unlike earthly kingdoms, which can be observed and analyzed and evaluated and explained, the Kingdom of the Church contains an essential element which defies human comprehension. It is that divine element which makes the Church ultimately a mystery, even to believers. Its growth, survival, and perpetual fecundity in the face of all odds will ever be a source of wonder, like the tiny mustard seed which is out of all physical proportion to the tree which springs from it. The inner dynamism of the Church is as baffling as the action of yeast in dough was to Jesus' hearers, who knew nothing of the chemistry of cell division. The Kingdom will in the course of history embrace all kinds of men, wheat and weeds, good and bad fish, saints and sinners. All will have a chance to attain to eternal salvation; it will be for the King Himself to judge in His own good time who has succeeded and who has failed.

Jesus taught all sorts of lessons in parable form: the spiritual nature of the Kingdom, its universality, the mercy of God, His love for sinners, man's duties to God, to himself, and to his neighbor, ever so many vital truths pointing the way to the salvation He would win for the souls He loved with an infinite love. And since love is patient and kind, Jesus was infinitely patient and kind in leading His lost brothers to the truth that would make them free.

XV

JESUS SHOWS HIS POWER
AND REVEALS HIS IDENTITY

St. Augustine once remarked: "Since Christ is the Word of God, His action is a word for us." Jesus taught not only orally, in conventional sermon and parable form; He was Himself a living Sermon, the Revelation of the Father. What He was spoke more loudly than what He said. His utter sinlessness, His mercy, gentleness, serenity, poverty, selfless love: these were the ultimate proof of His identity. One might shut one's eyes to His miracles or try smugly to explain them away, but it was impossible to explain Him away. His enemies eventually realized this and arrived at the only final solution to their dilemma: His murder.

Still, the miracles of Jesus form such an integral part of His story that without them it becomes completely incoherent, even nonsensical. Not that He was what one would call a wonder-worker. From the very outset of His mission He absolutely refused to use His power for His own benefit or simply to dazzle His contemporaries. Satan suggested that He do so and was sent packing. The divine Teacher used miracles for their pedagogical value, as vehicles of revelation. And what did they reveal? His power, certainly, but not exclusively by any means. Even His extraordinary displays of control over the forces of nature, like the stilling of the storm on the lake, or the change of water into wine, or the feeding of the multitudes — even these were motivated by sympathy, compassion, love, and were manifestations of these attractive virtues even more than of superhuman power. ·

Jesus came not to dazzle but to save, and it was faith in Him that would save, from the subjective point of view. His miracles served as a partial motive for that saving faith. Objectively they demonstrated that He had the power to save. It is especially significant that most of His miracles manifested His power over disease and death. These latter were linked in the minds of the people with sin; how often they are associated with diabolic possession! They were the province of Satan, through whom they had entered the human scene. Jesus' miracles of healing and His raising of the dead to life indicated clearly that He had power over Satan, that He had come to break his empire, to crush his head. This was the role they played in salvation history.

As motives of credibility the miracles are invaluable for proving Jesus' divine mission, and the Church has insisted on their importance in her traditional apologetics. Yet they by no means compel assent; they never did. Think of all the hundreds, even thousands, of people who witnessed them with their own eyes, as in the multiplication of the loaves and fishes. How many of them came to believe? Only a handful of devoted disciples, and even they had only an incipient faith, a faith which the Crucifixion all but shattered. Only antecedent good will could dispose a person to appreciate the significance of a miracle; how often Jesus demanded faith of a suppliant before curing him. To comprehend all the implications of the miracles, specifically the divinity of the one who performed them, the light of divine faith was needed. For the divine simply cannot be grasped by the human. Certainly the disciples had all the good will in the world, but it was only in the light of their post-Resurrection, Pentecostal faith that they really and truly comprehended the divinity of the Savior. Of His messianic character they had grown sure; witness Peter's confession in Mark 8:30 and Luke 9:21.* But this was humanly observable and humanly demonstrable; it is not an essentially divine fact. Significantly, when Jesus asked the apostles who people thought He was, they answered: "John the Baptist; others, Elias; and others, one of the prophets" (Mark 8:28). And after He had stilled the tempest, their reaction was: *"What manner of man* is this, that even the wind and the sea obey him?" (Matt. 8:27).

The miracles, then, did not compel assent, but they did furnish the data on which the light of divine faith would one day shine with full brilliance. At that time their divine significance would become thrillingly clear. In the meantime they disposed the souls of men of good will for the reception of that faith and, in addition, fulfilled an immediate pedagogical purpose in an extraordinarily impressive manner. Each of them was, in a broad sense, a sacrament, an external physical sign of an inner, spiritual, reality.

An excellent example of this marvelous blending of the human and the divine is the stilling of the storm on the lake (Mark 4:35-40). Jesus had put in a long hard day of preaching, and when evening came He sent His audience home for supper,

---

* Matthew's version calls for further discussion beyond our immediate scope.

got into one of His disciples' fishing boats, and asked them to make for the opposite shore. Before they had gone very far He fell into a deep sleep. The day's work had exhausted Him, and the gentle rocking of the boat combined with fatigue to make Him irresistibly drowsy. He laid His head back on a seat cushion, sighed wearily, and slept. All of a sudden, as it so often happens on the Lake of Galilee, a squall struck. The wind, funneled through a break in the surrounding hills, whipped the water into a frenzy, and the disciples, who knew that lake like the palms of their hands, were badly frightened. So sound was the slumber of the Master that they had to shake Him into wakefulness and apprise Him of their peril. Rising to His full height on the pitching vessel, He imperiously commanded: "Peace, be still!" And the wind fell, and there came a great calm (Mark 4:39).

What a marvelous blending of the human and the divine! What could be more human than Jesus' exhaustion and deep sleep? What more divine than His control of the forces of nature? Is not this incident a most dramatic expression of the truth we profess rather prosaically, that Jesus is true God and true man?

In the category of miracles of healing, the cure of the paralytic at Capharnaum is a splendid illustration of the pedagogical value of the miracles. Our Lord was teaching in a house one day, and so great was the crowd that no one else could squeeze in the narrow door. Along came a little group carrying a paralytic on an improvised stretcher. They had heard of Jesus' sympathy for the sick and of His power in healing them. In high hopes, then, they drew near the house, but their hopes were dashed to the ground when they saw that they wouldn't be able to get anywhere near Jesus. One of them, more enterprising — or more determined — than the rest, hit upon an idea. Why not carry the poor fellow up the outside stairway, remove part of the roughly thatched roof, and lower him right into the middle of the room before Jesus? This they did, and one can imagine the consternation of the audience at this highly unusual interruption. Our Lord's reaction, however, was not one of consternation. Rather, He was deeply moved by the faith of these good, simple people.

His first words took everyone by surprise: "Man, thy sins are forgiven thee." He saw past the paralysis of the unfortunate man's limbs to the paralysis of his soul and decided to cure first the greater of the two ills. And in so doing He indicated yet again the true purpose of His mission. It was not to wipe out disease and death but to destroy sin, the only real obstacle to salvation. After He had completed His redemptive work, sickness continued to strike down even the innocent, but the power of sin was broken and men had at their disposal the means to avoid it, or at least to be freed of it should it enter their lives.

Our Savior's enemies, with the acumen of men bent on stalking their prey and waiting for the first sign of weakness, of faltering, of error, were sure He had maneuvered Himself into an indefensible position. Surely the fellow was going too far, arrogating to Himself divine powers; anyone with any sense would know that only God can forgive sins. Really, this was too much! But it was they who fell into the trap. Their objection boomeranged. Jesus read their thoughts and agreed with their premise: only God can forgive sins. He then proceeded to show them that He had that power — and they could draw their own conclusions. They could contend, of course, that talk was cheap, that anyone could say that he was forgiving someone's sins. But how could he prove that he had actually done so? One way would be by performing an incontestably clear miracle. Jesus chose this method. "But that you may know that the Son of Man has power on earth to forgive sins" — he said to the paralytic — "I say to thee, arise, take up thy pallet and go to thy house." The man stood up on the spot, picked up his stretcher, and pushed his way through the crowd, glorifying God and bursting with eagerness to get home and walk in his own front door.

What conclusions the spectators drew we are not told. Luke tells us that they were astonished and somewhat frightened, that they glorified God and exclaimed: "We have seen wonderful things today" (5:26). The early Church, however, reflected on this incident with penetrating eyes of faith and understood all its implications. Matthew's conclusion to the narrative suggests that the Church saw in this miracle not only a demonstration of Jesus' divine power but also the basis of a like power shared by the apostles and their successors: "But when the crowds saw it, they were struck with fear, and glorified God *who had given such power to men"* (9:8).

. In many ways, the most fascinating miracle account in the gospels is John's description of the cure of the man born blind. When the disciples saw him sitting begging by the side of the road, they asked the Master if his blindness was a punishment for his own sins or for those of his parents. (There was an opinion current in some rabbinical circles that an unborn child was capable of committing sin.) Jesus assured them that the affliction was not directly attributable to a sin on either side. He then took advantage of the situation to illustrate in a dramatic way that He had come to dispel the darkness of ignorance and sin and to flood the souls of men with the light of truth and faith: "As long as I am in the world, I am the light of the world" (9:5).

Now our Lord could have said quite simply, "Receive thy sight." Instead He chose a method which was in itself out of all proportion to the effect but by that very fact strikingly illustrative of the efficacy of the sacramental system He was to bequeath to His Church. In His action on this occasion we are quite justified in seeing a demonstration of the power of anointing and washing (the baptismal rite) for the production of the light of faith and grace in the soul. He made a little salve of earth and spittle and anointed the man's eyes; then He instructed him to go and wash in the Pool of Siloe. John rather pointedly interprets the name of the pool as "Sent." Jesus was "sent" into the world by His Father, and John apparently does not want us to miss the connection between the waters of Siloe and those of Him who was "sent": the waters of Baptism. The man returned from the pool with his sight restored.

There followed an inquisition which demonstrates the efforts Jesus' enemies made to discredit Him, to shut their eyes to the obvious, to explain away what they could not ignore. First, the man's neighbors preferred to believe that the man who now saw was not really the blind beggar they had known. "He only looks like him," they said. But he insisted, "I am he." They brought him to the Pharisees, who immediately ducked the issue by pointing out that Jesus could not have exercised any divine power, since He had performed all these actions on the Sabbath. Obviously, no one who violated the Sabbath rest could be in God's favor. But the fact remained: the man could see. So they summoned his parents to get positive identification, and they got it. With a wilful blindness more hideous than that which had darkened the life of the cured man, they fell to vilifying Jesus. They returned to their inquisition and the poor fellow had to tell his story over and over again while they waited desperately for him to slip up, to contradict himself, to give them some pretext for their incredulity. But he stood his ground admirably, and gave answers which must have infuriated them. To their positive assertion that Jesus was a sinner he replied quite calmly: "Whether he is a sinner, I do not know. One thing I do know, that whereas I was blind, now I see." When they compared Jesus unfavorably to Moses, whom they knew to have been sent by God, he came out with this devastating observation: "Why, herein is the marvel, that you do not know where he is from, and yet he opened my eyes. Now we know that God does not hear sinners; but if anyone is a worshipper of God, and does his will, him he hears. Not from the beginning of the world has it been heard that anyone opened the eyes of a man born blind. If this man were not from God, he could do nothing." Inescapable logic, but ill will and hatred are much stronger than logic, as the answer of the man's self-appointed judges shows: "Thou wast altogether born in sin, and dost thou teach us?" The pride which plunged humanity into misery was still at work and would refuse over and over again God's generous efforts to rescue it from that misery. Satan would not give up without a struggle.

There are three instances of Jesus' having raised people from the dead, marvelous exhibitions of divine power which seem to have been largely neutralized by men's ill will. But they stand as brilliant testimonies to those empowered by faith to look at them honestly and humbly bow to their profound significance. All three of them speak eloquently not only of Jesus' power, but of His compassion, His love, His tenderness. Power without love can be cold and selfish, even cruel; and love without power can be maddeningly frustrating. But divine power coupled with divine love! Words simply cannot do justice to this combination, for it is infinite, and words are finite.

When Jesus raised the little daughter of Jairus from the dead He remembered something even her parents had forgotten: that she had been sick for some time and that now, restored to life and full health, she was as hungry as any normal twelve-year-old. And He instructed her parents to give her something to eat. She was to Him not just an excuse for a display of power; she was a hungry little girl; she was a person. The same warm compassion shines forth in the raising of the widow's son. Before performing the miracle Jesus comforted the heartbroken woman with the heartfelt plea: "Don't cry." And when the dead man sat up and began to speak, Jesus "gave him to his mother" (Luke 7:15). On the occasion of the raising of Lazarus, Jesus Himself cried. He wasn't crying for Lazarus, for He knew that He would call him from the tomb in a few moments. It was the sight of Martha and Mary, weeping because they did not know what He was about to do, that cut Him to the quick — and the Son of God cried.

The Savior was to climax His earthly career by the miracle of miracles, His own resurrection from the dead. This above all was to be the burden of the apostolic witness, the cornerstone of their preaching. Ill-disposed men might claim that He cured sick bodies and revived corpses by some sort of magic or even by diabolic power. They might grasp at straws and insist that the corpses were not really corpses, that the "dead" people were only comatose or perhaps drugged. Jesus' own resurrection from the dead defied sterile rationalization. One accepted it or he didn't. But if he did, he had also to accept all its implications: that Jesus was indeed the Son of God come to redeem men from sin by His death and to give them a share in His risen glory, a share which would be a pledge and a beginning of the eternal salvation He had put once more within their reach.

XVI

JESUS REDEEMS MANKIND

"Having loved his own who were in the world, he loved them to the limit" (John 13:1). With these words St. John, the beloved disciple, opens his account of the Last Supper. God's love for sinful men was about to burst over the world in full tide; He was about to give His Son in sacrifice for man's redemption. Jesus had given so many proofs of love during His public ministry; now He was going to give the greatest proof of all: "Greater love than this no man has, that one lay down his life for his friends" (John 15:13). On the eve of His redeeming death He seemed especially eager to demonstrate His love as compellingly as possible. Hardly had they reclined on the banquet couches when He got up, wrapped a towel about His waist, took a basin, and went from one to the other washing their feet — something not even a Jewish slave could be forced to do against his will. The full impact of the gesture hit Peter and he protested vehemently, but to no avail. During the meal itself the Master opened His heart to them as He had never done before, and from its depths poured forth words of love, affection, tender concern, consolation, reassurance, promise. There could have been no more appropriate setting for the institution of the Holy Eucharist, the Sacrament of Love, the Memorial of the Passion, the gift of Himself which He would go on giving until the end of time.

Jesus would have liked to prolong this last meal indefinitely, but His hour was at hand, that hour for which He had yearned with all His heart but which now filled that heart with unimaginable terror. Across the brook called Cedron, on a slope just opposite the temple, was an olive grove called Gethsemane ("oil press"). It was hither that He now led His little band. Leaving eight of them at the entrance to the garden — Judas had left the supper early to arrange for his Master's arrest — He took Peter, James, and John with Him and asked them to stay near Him while He prayed. "My soul is sad, even unto death," He confided to them, and this admission must have made them shudder.

We shall never know just how sad His soul was, how depressed and dispirited and fearful. He willed to die for men, to taste death in all its bitterness, and surely one of the most agonizing aspects of death is the anticipation of the suffering it will entail. If this is true under ordinary circumstances, what must it have been like in Jesus' case? His death was to be no ordinary one, but a protracted and horrible slaughter. He foresaw the punching, the spitting, the scourging, the crowning with thorns, the carrying of the cross. He could hear the sickening thud of hammer on nail as He was fixed to one of the most inhuman instruments of torture ever devised by man; He knew what the maddening thirst would be like, the strangling asphyxiation. His human soul was aghast at the prospect and He cried out to the Father for respite, for some mitigation of the rigors demanded by outraged divine justice. The physical agony He faced was bad enough, but the emotional torment was even worse. For He knew that millions of souls in the course of history would spurn His love, would refuse the grace He was about to win for them at such a price. His heart was close to breaking as He pictured one of His own betraying Him with a hypocritical kiss and hurling himself into the abyss. And on another level He heard Peter denying Him three times and saw all but John deserting Him in selfish terror. It was an experience almost beyond human endurance, an experience which forced the blood through His pores to run down His face like beads of sweat. It wrung from His twisted lips the tortured cry: "O Father, if it be possible, let this chalice pass from me." But in the same anguished breath came that magnificent acceptance of the divine will — whatever that will might decree: "Not my will, but thine be done." Who will ever know what it cost the human nature of Christ to utter those few words? No one; but they do help us to appreciate the love of Jesus for sinners. He would suffer anything to save them.

Already His disciples, insensitive to the struggle He was enduring, had fallen asleep in the cool dark of the garden. He felt so utterly alone. But He was calm now; the crisis was past and He knew what He must do. Lights were bobbing along in the valley and drawing nearer to Gethsemane. His hour had come. It was not long before Judas strode into the garden at the head of a band of armed guards, walked up to Him, and kissed Him — the signal He had given the soldiers in advance. But Jesus, pursuing Him with love right to the end, said quite simply, "Friend, for what purpose hast thou come?" And oh, the sorrow in that word, "Friend"! The treacherous Judas had been true to form, and now the impetuous Peter did something equally characteristic. He drew his dagger, swung wildly in the flickering light, and slashed off the ear of a servant of the high priest. And just as characteristically, Jesus healed the wound. The disciples, now completely awake to the situation, took to their heels.

Bound like a common criminal, Jesus was led to a cell in the palace of the high priest to await trial. Caiphas was the actual high priest, but his father-in-law Annas, who had been deposed from the high priesthood by the Romans, still wielded considerable influence. It is likely that they both had apartments in the same palace and that Jesus could be led easily across a courtyard from the one to the other. Of His appearance before

Annas we know little but the fact; of His trial before Caiphas we are quite well informed. Caiphas was a political opportunist; he held on to his office for eighteen years, from 18 to 36, by staying on the right side of the Romans. A troublemaker like Jesus might easily have upset his applecart. It was imperative that he be put out of circulation.

Jewish law required that trials involving capital punishment take place only in the daytime, and as soon as day broke the Sanhedrin, the Supreme Court, passed sentence. But it seems that this was a legal fiction and that the trial actually took place during the night or early morning hours. Jesus was led from the home of Annas across the courtyard to that of the wily Caiphas, where the Sanhedrists had hastily gathered. The trial was a farce. The high priest asked Jesus about His teaching and He replied that there was no secret about it; He had been preaching openly in public places and anyone who had heard Him could answer the high priest's question. This answer won for Him a sharp slap in the face from one of the officers of the court, a foretaste of the indignities He was to suffer as the day wore on. Witnesses were summoned, but their testimony was contradictory. Frustrated, Caiphas broke all the rules by asking the prisoner to testify against Himself. "I adjure you by the living God that thou tell us whether thou art the Christ, the Son of God." And Jesus answered: "Thou hast said it. Nevertheless, I say to you, hereafter you shall see the Son of Man sitting at the right hand of the Power and coming upon the clouds of heaven." Caiphas could hardly have hoped for a more unequivocal answer. He tore his robe in a gesture of horror and declared Jesus guilty of blasphemy. The court decreed that He pay the full penalty for the crime: death, and proceeded to spit in His face and pummel Him. Was it not enough that He was to die? Why this unnecessarily crude conduct? Did they really hate Him so, Him who stood as a living reproach to their behavior?

Meanwhile Peter had mustered up enough courage to venture into the courtyard where he could pick up news of the proceedings. But that was as far as his courage took him. He was really quite apprehensive, since Jesus was obviously in serious trouble and he had been an intimate of His. One of the palace maids spotted him and let him know that she recognized him. He told her she didn't know what she was talking about and moved to a safer spot near the gate. But another sharp-eyed maid caught sight of him and announced his identity to the bystanders. Frantic, Peter swore, "I don't know the man!" But the bystanders were curious now and pressed in on him, remarking on his Galilean accent. Cursing and swearing he disclaimed any connection with the Master. At that very moment a cock crowed. Startled, he remembered Jesus' prophecy that before the cock crowed he would have denied Him three times. Realizing what he had done, he left the courtyard, and in the dismal predawn darkness, cried his heart out.

Another apostle was having even more serious trouble. Judas, too, recognized the heinousness of his crime and tried to soothe his tortured conscience by returning the blood-money to the authorities who had used him so shamefully. They treated him with the contempt he deserved. Plunged into despair, he took his own life.

After the court had "legally" passed sentence at dawn, they bound Jesus and brought Him to the procurator, Pontius Pilate. The Romans would not allow them to inflict the death penalty without the approval of the procurator. The Jewish leaders knew Pilate like a book, knew precisely where he was vulnerable. He was there to protect the interests of the Empire, and nothing so threatened those interests as seriously as rebellion. Therefore they accused Jesus of advocating nonpayment of taxes and of claiming to be king of the Jews, a claim which, under the circumstances, was tantamount to high treason. Jesus admitted that He was indeed a king, but hastened to assure Pilate that His kingship was of a sort which posed no threat to Roman domination. Pilate apparently got the impression that the prisoner was a bit unbalanced, a harmless fool whom the Jews were taking much too seriously. He made it quite obvious that he did not consider Him deserving of death and used every subterfuge at his disposal to avoid handing down a decision.

Hearing that Jesus was a Galilean and knowing that Herod, the tetrarch of Galilee, was in Jerusalem for the Passover, he sent Him to the Jewish ruler's residence, hoping to be relieved of responsibility in the affair. Herod, however, had no intention of taking sides. He had heard a great deal about Jesus' activity in Galilee but had never seen Him. And now here He was, and Herod saw a chance to enjoy the services of a court jester for a while. The miracles of which he had heard he had shrugged off as the clever tricks of a charlatan; now he would see for himself. But to all his cajoleries Jesus answered not a word. Determined to make Him play the fool and nettled by His lack of response, he had his soldiers dress Him in the robe of a clown, and after they had tired of making sport of Him, sent Him back to Pilate.

The procurator announced that he had found no reason to condemn the prisoner and that Herod had not either. He would release Him. But the Jews were not going to be robbed of their prey so easily. They reminded Pilate of the custom of releasing a prisoner at Passover time; they would take Barabbas, an anarchist and murderer, and give Jesus to the state in exchange. Seeing through this obvious ruse, Pilate made another move to set Jesus free. The attempt was met with frenzied cries of "Crucify him!" In a desperate appeal to their mercy, Pilate decided to have Jesus scourged. He hoped that when they saw the effects of this treatment their lust for blood would be sated and they would drop the case. For the Roman scourge did unspeakable things to a man. Not only did it cause welts and abrasions. It was manufactured of leather thongs with pieces of metal attached to the ends. These prongs tore into the flesh and ripped it away in strips. Often enough it sufficed to cause death. Jesus survived, but He must have been a pitiable spectacle indeed. The soldiers who assisted at the savage lashing knew no pity. When it was over they threw a purple cloak about His bleeding shoulders, made a rough crown from the thorny branches they used for kindling their fires, and mocked Him contemptuously as King of the Jews. And as if He hadn't been beaten enough, they punctuated their mockery with vicious slaps.

The Jews proved to have no more pity than the pagan soldiery. Completely unmoved, they insisted that Jesus be crucified. Finally they played their trump card: "If thou release this man, thou art no friend of Caesar; for everyone who makes himself king sets himself against Caesar." The threat implied in these words was well calculated to strike terror into the heart of a man in Pilate's position, and he bowed before it. He had already literally washed his hands of the affair, and now, in a futile gesture of spite, he ordered that a placard be affixed to Jesus' cross with the inscription: "Jesus of Nazareth, King of the Jews."

There is no need to dwell on the horrors of the crucifixion. It was a method of execution so inhumanly brutal that a Roman citizen could under no circumstances be subjected to it. It was reserved for slaves; and so the King of Kings died a slave's death to free men from slavery. But before He died, He gave final evidence of His consuming love. He prayed His Father to forgive the very men who had driven the nails through His hands and feet and were callously casting lots for His clothes. He promised the penitent thief, one of the two malefactors between whom He was crucified, a place in heaven. He gave to all men, in the person of St. John, His last and most precious possession: His own mother. And then, having no more to give, He cried out to His Father, bowed His head, and died. It was finished.

Born in a hillside cave, Jesus was buried in one. As a birth-place, a strange cave was a mark of poverty and humility; as a burial place, a stranger's cave was a mark of poverty but also a sign of reverence and respect. For only the well-to-do could afford such tombs, at least in the region of Jerusalem. Joseph of Arimathea, a member of the Sanhedrin who had taken no part in their dastardly deliberations, was an admirer of Jesus. He got permission to bury Him. In the meantime, a Roman soldier had made sure of Jesus' death by plunging his spear into His already broken heart. Since it was the time of preparation for the Sabbath, there was no opportunity to prepare the body for burial with the usual ointments and spices. It was merely wrapped in a linen cloth and laid on a slab in the burial chamber. Then a large circular stone was rolled in its groove across the low opening to the cave.

. Very early on the first day of the week some devoted women came to complete the burial ritual. When they were almost there, they remembered the stone and realized with dismay that not even all of them together could as much as budge it. Much to their surprise they found the stone already rolled back from the entrance to what they soon discovered to be the empty tomb. Not quite empty — there was a young man there in dazzling attire who informed them that Jesus had risen. The guards whom the Jews had posted were nowhere in sight. They had run into town to report the resurrection and were promptly bribed to keep quiet and, if questioned, to say that the disciples had stolen the body while they were asleep — a ridiculous alibi if there ever was one.

The women ran to the apostles and arrived, all out of breath, to tell them the good news. And the apostles treated them like hysterical women — all but Peter and John, who rushed to the tomb to see for themselves. Mary Magdalen had been unable to tear herself away from the place, and when she saw someone standing near her, she did not recognize Him through her tears. She thought it was the caretaker until He spoke her name, "Mary!" And all she could say was "Rabboni" (Master)! Jesus appeared to others that same day: to Peter, the two disciples on the road to Emmaus, and to all the assembled apostles except the absent Thomas, who would not accept even their testimony. A week later, when Thomas was present, Jesus appeared to them again and wrung from the heart of His incredulous disciple that magnificent profession of faith, "My Lord and my God!"

Throughout a period of forty days Jesus appeared frequently to the disciples in various places, giving them final instructions in the conduct of the Church and advising them to remain in the Holy City until He should send the Holy Spirit upon them. At the end of this period He ascended visibly into heaven from the Mount of Olives. The scene of His cruelest desolation thus became the scene of His definitive glorification.

XVII

JESUS FOUNDS THE KINGDOM
AND RATIFIES THE NEW COVENANT

By His passion, death, and resurrection, the Savior redeemed mankind. It was for this purpose that He had come to earth in fulfillment of a plan motivated by divine love and devised by divine ingenuity. The sin which had made redemption necessary, though committed by two finite creatures, was directed against an infinite God and was consequently quasi-infinite. It put men infinitely in His debt and no finite creature could ever pay off such a debt. There was need of a mediator who would adequately represent both parties: sinful man and the God he had offended. The incarnate Son of God answered this need perfectly: with man He shared a perfect human nature; as the second Person of the Blessed Trinity He was perfectly one with God. In Him heaven and earth, God and man, were joined in a unique manner. As a result of this ineffable union, everything He did as man He did also as God. Every action of His was accordingly the action of an infinite Person and hence infinitely valuable. The satisfaction He offered by His death on the cross wiped out mankind's staggering debt to the Father. That sacrifice was also infinitely meritorious, winning for all men of all time the grace to return to their privileged position as children of God and heirs of the Kingdom which He had prepared for them from all eternity.

Just as God respected the freedom of our first parents, so He respects the freedom of all His children. He will force salvation on no one. Each one must desire it and take the means established by God to attain to it. The eternal plan, then, called for the preparation of clear, objective means to salvation, means suited to man's nature. Salvation history culminated on Calvary; it did not end there. It continues until the end of time, as long as there are souls to be saved. It continues in the Kingdom of the Church, established by the Savior as the means offered to all men of good will.

Jesus' mission centered on the foundation of this Kingdom. Both St. John the Baptist and He opened their ministries with a proclamation that the Kingdom of Heaven was at hand. His subsequent activity aimed at forming the Kingdom, training its personnel, explaining its precise nature and function, giving rules for its organization and conduct. One of His first concerns was to select the personnel which would make up its nucleus. Not long after the baptism which inaugurated His messianic career, He selected a first group: Andrew, John, Simon Peter, Philip, and Nathanael (Bartholomew). They did not at first remain with Him exclusively, but after a while He extended to them a definitive call and they accepted. Others received the call, too, and soon the roster was complete: Simon Peter, James and John, the sons of Zebedee, Andrew, Philip, Bartholomew, Matthew, Thomas, James, the son of Alpheus, Jude Thaddeus, Simon the Cananean, and Judas Iscariot.

They were a rather ordinary group of men of the working class. They included several fishermen and a tax collector. While they were not well-to-do, they were not paupers either. The fishermen among them owned their own equipment and apparently did a fair business. While they do not seem to have received much formal education, it would be unfair to class them as illiterate. They gave evidence of being natively intelligent and interested in learning. As a group, then, they were simple,

manly, sincere, conscientious workmen, generous and good-
hearted. But they had their faults, too: incredulity, obtuseness,
ambition, timidity, even faithlessness. Peter himself is depicted
as headstrong and impetuous, a boaster, a quitter, a coward.
And of course they all shared the erroneous views of their co-
religionists regarding the Messiah and His kingdom.

. These were the men Jesus set about training to continue
His work on earth, and He kept at it patiently all throughout
His public life. They were with Him day and night, watching,
listening, questioning, imitating, learning in the school of the
Master. St. Matthew gives us, as we have seen, a magnificent
synthesis of Jesus' instructions on the nature and conduct of
the Kingdom. The first of the great discourses, the Sermon on
the Mount, established the basic charter of the Kingdom, out-
lining the personal and social qualities which would be required
of its members. The apostles, seated directly before Him, would
realize that if the ordinary Christian was to be the salt of the
earth and the light of the world, they who were so intimately
associated with the Master would have to be so to an even
higher degree. All of these strange but wonderful new teachings
of Jesus would have made a much deeper impression on them
than on the audience at large.

In the second discourse (Matt. 9:37 — 10:42) we have an
excellent example of instructions given directly to the apostles.
Realizing the value of "field work," Jesus sent them out on a
trial preaching mission. They were to proclaim the advent of
the Kingdom, and to help them in their preaching, He gave
them a share in His miraculous powers. His instruction to them
is really far-reaching advice on the spread of the Kingdom
throughout the world. It transcends the narrow confines of
Palestine and looks to other places and other times. Their task
will not be easy, and He tells them so quite frankly. He is
sending them out like sheep among a pack of wolves. They
must therefore be as wise as serpents while preserving the
innocence of doves. They will be scourged by the Jews in their
synagogues and hailed before pagan governors and kings. But

let them not worry about what they shall say in their defense; the Holy Spirit will be with them, strengthening, encouraging, enlightening.

Persecution and hatred will plague them as they go through the world. Hatred will breed treachery even within the same household, with brother betraying brother, fathers handing their children over to the authorities, and children doing the same to their parents. And really, this is what they should expect, for they are no better than He, and He has been the object of constant, bitter hatred. Still, they must not be afraid. Courageously they must speak out, confident of God's protection. Even should they have to suffer martyrdom, they should rejoice in the rich reward that awaits them. His own coming has created an inevitable tension in the world; so will theirs. They must accept this tension and live it bravely, with complete detachment from the interests and standards of the world, even from the closest ties of natural affection. In other words, they must follow the path He is blazing, the way of the Cross. Thus did the King forewarn and forearm the soldiers who were to extend His kingdom to the end of the world.

If anyone needed a clear understanding of the nature of that Kingdom, it was surely those who would be responsible for its conduct, and St. Matthew gives us in chapter 13 a series of parables which stress the mystery of the Kingdom. The apostles must not be dismayed if the Kingdom does not seem to operate according to the ordinary rules. For it contains a supernatural element as well as a natural one: it will be divine as well as human. Right at the beginning of this chapter we have an excellent example of the special care Jesus took in the instruction of His chosen ones. After telling the crowds the parable of the sower, He took the disciples aside and gave them a clear and detailed explanation of it. In the parable of the weeds He warned them not to get upset if sinners cropped up in the Church. After all, it would be its mission precisely to save sinners, and if they did not respond, then at harvest time the Judge would mete out to them their deserved punishment. They must not be dismayed at the "human element" in the Church. This parable, too, He explained to them at their request, and reinforced its lesson with the parable of the net enclosing both good and bad fish.

Another section of Matthew's gospel, the Gospel of the Church, presents much interesting material on the organization of the Kingdom (13:54 — 19:1). In this section Peter stands out prominently. He is promised primacy over the Church, is reproved by Jesus for objecting to His prophecy of the Passion, is a privileged witness of the Transfiguration, finds the coin in the fish's mouth and uses it to pay the temple tax for himself and Jesus, inquires and is given instructions on the forgiveness of enemies. Jesus instructs the apostles on the need of prayer and fasting to perform an exorcism. Two incidents of Jesus' feeding the multitude underscore prophetically the place of the Eucharist in the Church. The apostles are warned against ambition, a fault to which they were not strangers. In their work for souls they must neglect no one: they may have ninety-nine sheep safely in the fold, but must still go in search of that one stray. His advice on fraternal correction gives clear teaching on the judiciary powers of the Church, including the power of excommunication (18:15-18).

Within the Church there were to be specific rites channeling to individual souls the inner life of the Kingdom, the grace merited by the Savior in His redemptive act. Jesus' teaching on the necessity of Baptism is clear and unequivocal: "Amen, amen, I say to thee, unless a man be born again of water and the Spirit, he cannot enter into the kingdom of God" (John 3:5). But the sacrament *par excellence* was to be the Eucharist, in which Jesus would give His very self to men so as to unite them with Himself and with one another in an intimate union of loving mutual possession. It would be a direct communication to the human soul of the very source of grace, the Savior Himself, imparting His merits, His life.

A great deal of preparation was necessary to dispose men for the acceptance of such a stupendous notion. The multiplication of the loaves was one such preparation. St. John has rendered us invaluable service in giving us Jesus' express explanation of one such multiplication (John 6). Significantly, our Lord begins by demanding that His listeners have faith in Him as the bread come down from heaven. One who cannot accept the Incarnation will never accept the Eucharist. "I am the bread of life. . . . For I have come down from heaven, not to do my will, but the will of him who sent me. . . . For this is the will of my Father who sent me, that whoever beholds the Son, and believes in him, shall have everlasting life, and I will raise him up on the last day. . . . Amen, amen, I say to you, he who believes in me has life everlasting."

Then He switches to the Eucharist itself. "I am the bread of life. . . . I am the living bread that has come down from heaven. If anyone eat of this bread he shall live forever; and the bread that I will give is my flesh for the life of the world. . . . He who eats my flesh and drinks my blood has life everlasting and I will raise him up on the last day. For my flesh is food indeed, and my blood is drink indeed. He who eats my flesh, and drinks my blood, abides in me and I in him. As the living Father has sent me, and as I live because of the Father, so he who eats me, he shall also live because of me."

John tells us that many of the disciples found this doctrine utterly fantastic. They turned away and no longer went about with Him. He was sad at their departure, of course, but He did not water down His teaching to retain them. Indeed, He turned to the apostles themselves and asked, "Do you also wish to go away?" To which Peter answered, "Lord, to whom shall we go? Thou hast words of eternal life. . . ."

The minds of the apostles were prepared, then, for the actual institution of the Eucharist at the Last Supper, and they expressed no surprise when Jesus offered them bread and said, "This is my body," and then a cup of wine with the words, "This is my blood." The Church now had its great Sacrament, which its ministers were to distribute to the faithful. For after having celebrated the first Mass and distributed Communion for the first time, Jesus commanded His apostles, "Do this in commemoration of me." They were now priests. But there are words other than these essential ones which are rich in significance for a study of salvation history.

In consecrating the wine, Jesus said, "This is my *blood of the new covenant,* which is being shed for many unto the forgiveness of sins." The focal point of salvation history in the old dispensation was the establishment of the Covenant on Mt. Sinai by which Israel became God's own people, a community apart, "a kingdom of priests, a holy nation" (Ex. 19:6). The "church" of the Old Testament was thereby formally constituted. After a sacrifice had been offered to Yahweh in ratification of the Covenant, Moses took the blood of the sacrificial animals and put half of it in large bowls. The other half he poured on the altar. Then he sprinkled the people with the contents of the bowls.

And now Jesus was instituting the New and Eternal Covenant, forming a new Israel, a new people of God, a new Church. He would ratify this Covenant by the shedding of His own precious blood, which would be poured out on the altar of Calvary and, through the Eucharist, "sprinkled" on all the members of the new community. As High Priest of the New Law, He ordained the first of those priests who would share His eternal priesthood and make His sacrifice, through their own priestly activity and that of their successors, immediately efficacious for the sanctification of all those who, until the end of time, would draw near the Eucharistic altar.

The Sinaitic Covenant was sealed within the framework of the Exodus, which had begun with the sacrifice of the Paschal Lamb. The New Covenant was sealed in connection with the renewal of that sacrifice, the feast of the Passover. Thus another great saving act of God was given its transcendent realization in *the* saving act accomplished by His Son. The blood of the paschal lamb, sprinkled on the doorposts of the Israelites, had saved their first-born from that death which constituted the horror of the tenth plague. The blood of the Lamb of God delivered all men who would avail themselves of its power from the death of sin and the definitive death of eternal damnation. St. John, who was especially aware of the paschal aspect of the redemption, reflected on the detail of the soldiers' not breaking Jesus' legs to insure His death, and was reminded of a prescription regarding the preparation of the lamb for the paschal meal: "Not a bone of his shall you break" (John 19:36). And St. Peter expresses this whole profound concept most eloquently as follows: "You know that you were redeemed from the vain manner of life handed down from your fathers, not with perishable things, with silver or gold, but with the precious blood of Christ, as of a lamb without blemish and without spot (1 Pet. 1:18-19).

XVIII

JESUS ORGANIZES THE KINGDOM

AND PROCLAIMS ITS MISSION

It was after the resurrection that Jesus, in the fullness of His risen power and glory, put the finishing touches on the organization of His Kingdom. The Church was to continue His mission of salvation in the world; through it He would conduct salvation history to its glorious term in eternity. To this end He conferred upon His apostles those final powers of jurisdiction and sanctification which they would need to accomplish their mission. True, during His lifetime He had carefully and pains-takingly instructed them in the nature and conduct of the Kingdom. He had promised to grant them certain powers and had indicated what their attitude to and use of them should be. And on His last night with them He had ordained them priests, empowering and commanding them to offer the Eucharistic sacrifice, the memorial of the Passion and the channel of its graces and merits.

All was not finished, however. St. Luke tells us that "he showed himself alive after his passion by many proofs, during forty days appearing to them and speaking of the kingdom of God" (Acts 1:3). The Greek text is a bit more explicit here. Translated quite literally it says: "speaking the things concerning the kingdom of God." Jesus, then, during these forty days preceding His visible departure from them, spoke to them often of matters concerning the Church. We have no way of knowing everything He discussed with them, but the gospels have recorded a few very illuminating examples.

First of all, He wanted to give the Church a clearly defined hierarchical structure. Divine organization though it was, it was to be human, too, composed of men living in a very real world and offered to the world as a visible, objective means of salvation. No human organization can survive without order, without duly established authority. Jesus had no illusions about human nature, even human nature elevated by grace. Accordingly, He definitively appointed Simon Peter to rule the new community with supreme power of jurisdiction over all its members.

It may seem strange to consider in this post-Resurrection setting the event which St. Matthew records within the framework of our Lord's public ministry: Peter's confession of Jesus' divinity and his receiving of the primacy. There is, however, a rather strong opinion that this confession could have been made only in the light of the Resurrection and that its present position in Matthew's gospel is to be explained by that Evangelist's obvious synthetic method of composition. His clearly discernible disregard for the chronology of Jesus' words and deeds is axiomatic, his concern for logical grouping equally so. Even a hasty comparison of his presentation with that of Mark and Luke will show why. In this particular instance, Mark and Luke both record the event which took place at Caesarea Philippi, but both of them give a much shorter version of Peter's confession: "Thou art the Christ" (Mark 8:29); "the Christ of God" (Luke 9:20). And they have no mention of the conferring of the primacy at this point. Interestingly enough, even in Matthew's account, our Lord brings the incident to a close with a strict order to the disciples "to tell no one that he was Jesus *the Christ*" (16:20). It is quite possible that Matthew, following his accustomed method of logical grouping, filled out the incident with another, fuller, confession of Peter from the period after the Resurrection, the profession of faith which occasioned the bestowal of the primacy. This view has much to recommend it, and while it is far from certain, it is probable enough to warrant our putting the incident in the present context. Of course, regardless of its historical context, it retains its full force.

"I say to thee, thou art Peter (Rock), and upon this rock I will build my Church, and the gates of hell shall not prevail against it. And I will give thee the keys of the kingdom of heaven; and whatever thou shalt bind on earth shall be bound in heaven, and whatever thou shalt loose on earth shall be loosed in heaven" (Matt. 16:18-19). The change of the apostle's name was significant in itself, indicating that he enjoyed a very special relationship with Jesus. The new name defined that relationship. He was to be the solid foundation on which the Church would be built, the center of its unity; and all the forces of hell would be powerless against it. Under the familiar figures of "keys" and "binding and loosing" Jesus conferred on Peter supreme jurisdictional and doctrinal authority in the Church, assuring him that his decisions would be ratified by heaven.

In the course of the Last Supper, just before His prediction of Peter's triple denial, our Lord had said to him, "Simon, Simon, behold, Satan has desired to have you, that he may sift you as wheat. But I have prayed for thee, that thy faith may not fail; and do thou, when once thou hast turned again, strengthen thy brethren" (Luke 22:31-32). Peter did falter during the Passion, but almost immediately "turned again" and wept bitter tears of repentance. Now his brethren could look to the Rock for strength and guidance. The account of his activity in the early Church shows that he did not betray the trust reposed in him.

St. John gives us another account of Jesus' commission to Peter as head of the Church. The setting was the very familiar one of the shore of the Lake of Galilee. The risen Savior had appeared on the beach as the disciples were about to give up after a discouraging night of fishing. Quite a few of the apostles were there: Peter, Thomas, Nathanael, James and John, and two others whose names are not given. Following the Lord's directions, they made quite a catch; John remembered the exact number: one hundred and fifty-three. They breakfasted together on some of the fish and then Jesus said to Simon Peter: "Simon, son of John, dost thou love me more than these do?" He said to him, "Yes, Lord, thou knowest that I love thee." He said to him, "Feed my lambs." He said to him a second time, "Simon, son of John, dost thou love me?" He said to him, "Yes, Lord, thou knowest that I love thee." He said to him, 'Feed my lambs." A third time he said to him, "Simon, son of John, dost thou love me?" Peter was grieved because he said to him for the third time, "Dost thou love me?" And he said to him, "Lord, thou knowest all things, thou knowest that I love thee." He said to him, "Feed my sheep" (John 21:15-17). In this touching scene, Jesus made Peter the supreme shepherd of His flock and commissioned him to feed all, not just the lambs, but the sheep too. Those in authority in the Church as well as the vast throngs of the faithful are to look trustingly to Peter for the truth that will nourish and sustain their faith. They will trust him and obey him with the simple confidence of sheep in their shepherd. Jesus had already painted a beautiful picture of Himself as the Good Shepherd (John 10:1-21); Peter is to exercise the same authority over His sheep and show the same warm concern for them as He had done and would continue to do.

During this same post-Resurrection period our Lord conferred upon His apostles another power which was to play an extremely important part in the work of the Church, the power to forgive sins. The Church was to continue the battle against sin which He had waged so consistently and had won so definitively by His death and resurrection. The fruits of His victory must be passed on to individual souls throughout the rest of salvation history. Accordingly, on the very afternoon of His resurrection He appeared to the apostles gathered in the upper room and said to them, "Peace be to you! As the Father has sent me, I also send you." When he had said this, he breathed upon them, and said to them, "Receive the Holy Spirit; whose sins you shall forgive, they are forgiven them; and whose sins you shall retain, they are retained" (John 20: 21-23).

These are just some of the steps Jesus took to give definite structure to His Church during the days after His resurrection. It is likely that He touched on many other subjects in the course of the forty days during which He appeared to them and discussed matters concerning the Kingdom. But now the time of His final leavetaking was drawing near, time for the final instructions, the final solemn commissions. The different gospels give different versions of the final scene, although they all agree substantially. Mark's is very clear, direct, and reassuring: "Go into the whole world and preach the gospel to every creature. He who believes and is baptized shall be saved, but he who does not believe shall be condemned. And these signs shall attend those who believe: in my name they shall cast out devils; they shall speak in new tongues; they shall take up serpents; and if they drink any deadly thing, it shall not hurt them; they shall lay hands upon the sick and they shall get well" (16:15-18). Matthew tells of an appearance in Galilee, and the words which He addressed to the apostles on that occasion have become classic: "All power in heaven and on earth has been given to me. Go, therefore, and make disciples of all nations, baptizing them in the name of the Father and of the Son and of the Holy Spirit, teaching them to observe all that I have commanded you; and behold I am with you all days even unto the consummation of the world" (28:18-20).

Here is a clear statement of the Church's authority and of its mission. That authority comes from none other than Jesus, brilliantly manifested as Son-of-God-in-power by His resurrection from the dead (Rom. 1:4). The mission of the Church is universal; the apostles are to initiate all nations into the Kingdom by means of Baptism in the name of the most Holy Trinity. And if Jesus is truly the Son of God, then all of His commandments must be obeyed as means of attaining eternal salvation. The Church, then, has a divinely imposed duty to teach all men to observe these commands. Men may balk at some of them as "unreasonable" or "impractical." The Church has no choice in the matter; it has a divine mandate to carry out. Though the forces of evil may rebel and attack with diabolical fury, the Church can stand firm with supreme confidence, for He to whom all power in heaven and on earth has been given has promised to be with it all days, even to the consummation of the world, until the last glorious chapter of salvation history will have been written.

There remained, however, one more act to be accomplished in the present phase of that history, the descent of the Holy Spirit. It was He, so clearly promised by Jesus, who would enlighten the disciples with the light of divine faith and enrich their souls with the supernatural gifts which would enable them to carry out their superhuman mission. In Acts 1:8 St. Luke incorporates the promise into his account of Jesus' last words on the Mount of the Ascension: "You shall receive power when the Holy Spirit comes upon you, and you shall be witnesses for me in Jerusalem and in all Judea and Samaria and even to the very ends of the earth." Again the universal mission of the Church and the promise of power to carry it out. The promise was fulfilled and the mission has been carried out—magnificently.

XIX

THE GROWTH OF THE
KINGDOM OF GOD ON EARTH

The Church which Jesus left in the world counted only about one hundred and twenty souls. At the center was Peter, and, linking them most closely with Jesus was Mary, His Mother. This little group was quite thoroughly Jewish, rooted in a past from which providentially guided circumstances would have to wrench them, and the wrenching process would be a painful one. They remained faithful to the practices of Judaism and to the liturgy of the temple. Indeed, their piety attracted the admiration of their fellow Jews.

Still they *were* different. The descent of the Holy Spirit, which took place on the Jewish feast of Pentecost, only about ten days after Jesus' ascension, had wrought a profound change in their souls. As Jesus had promised (John 14:26), the Spirit had brought them the gifts of full and perfect faith, enlightening them with the supernatural knowledge to see deep into the Christ-event and to comprehend its divinely profound implications. This experience transformed their personalities, too. Whereas they had been timid and frightened, hiding away in the Upper Room "for fear of the Jews," now they appeared quite boldly in public and fearlessly spoke of Jesus as the Messiah who had risen from the dead and had entered into heavenly glory.

Some of their practices set them apart, too. They met frequently for liturgical services of their own and shared a common life. They demanded repentance and baptism in the name of Jesus as the first essential steps to salvation. Even so, it would have been hard to distinguish them from similar pious groups within orthodox Judaism. But the priestly aristocracy was uneasy nevertheless. These simple souls were actually glorifying him whom they had so recently condemned. What was worse, they were imitating him, even to the point of performing miracles. Attempts at intimidating them failed rather embarrassingly; they enjoyed public favor, and many sincere Pharisees and priests were joining their courageous company.

Thanks to the powerful grace of the Holy Spirit which accompanied the forthright preaching of Peter and his associates, the little community grew by leaps and bounds. In a matter of weeks, what had been a group of little more than a hundred became an organization of several thousand. It is amazing to note the rapidity with which the work of organization was accomplished. This touched many levels of activity: worship, instruction, contributions to a common fund, and the administration of that fund in works of charity. The apostles themselves, who realized that the most sacred charge laid upon them by Jesus was that of preaching, delegated administrative duties to others so as to be able to carry out their divine commission without distraction.

The essence of their preaching can be detected in their earliest sermons as recorded in the *Acts of the Apostles.* Using the traditional biblical terminology so familiar to them, they affirmed their belief that Jesus was "the Lord," seated in glory "at the right hand of God," and that power and glory were His by divine right. They expressed their belief by praying to Him as God; they baptized in His name and in His name performed miracles. They and their disciples were exultingly aware of having received the promised Spirit and could point to undeniably extraordinary manifestations of His presence within them.

Among the first converts to the infant Church was a large group of Jews from outside Palestine. They had either returned to their homeland to settle down or were on pilgrimage. Attracted by the dynamic preaching of the apostles they became fervent Christians. Their entrance into the Church created a certain friction. They had passed their lives in pagan countries; their language was Greek and so, to a great extent, was their culture. Not unexpectedly, they entertained rather broad views on many of the practices of Judaism and rather frankly considered them outmoded and unnecessary. This turned out to be providential, for sooner or later the Church would have to break completely with official Judaism. These "Hellenists" within her ranks sparked the transition.

It was from among this group that the seven deacons were chosen to assist the apostles in the administration of the Church's material affairs. One of them, Stephen, was especially zealous in trying to convert the Jews. His preaching infuriated them and he was arrested and brought before the Sanhedrin. There before that august body he fearlessly attacked them for their obstinate blindness to the truth and for their murder of Jesus. They could hardly believe their ears! His suggestion that the temple was on the way out laid him open to the capital charge of blasphemy. Enraged, they dragged him outside the city and savagely stoned him to death.

This touched off a persecution which forced many of the Christians to flee Jerusalem. But wherever they went they brought the Good News with them, and so the persecution actually furthered the expansion of the Church. Within a short time the Lord Jesus had been heralded all along the Mediterranean coast, as far north as the great metropolis of Antioch in Syria and even over on the island of Cyprus. Each new little community became, in its turn, a center of missionary activity. Jews who had been converted while on pilgrimage to the Holy City carried the message of salvation with them when they went back to their several homes, and the seed of the faith was planted in Damascus, Alexandria, and Rome.

The apostles themselves began to preach outside of the mother Church of Jerusalem. At Caesarea on the coast, Peter had an experience which was to prove of signal importance in the spread of the Church. In obedience to a mystical vision, he baptized a Gentile, a Roman centurion named Cornelius. This was a daring departure; the Jerusalem community was staunchly Jewish and shared the Jewish contempt for pagans. Peter needed a vision to encourage him to admit Cornelius, and he had to defend his action before the church of the Holy City. This was just the beginning of a problem which was to cause the Church much anguish in the years ahead.

Should Gentiles be accepted as Christians directly, or should they be made to enter by the vestibule of Judaism — specifically, by being circumcised? There was a serious division of opinion on this question, and the situation was growing more pressing. Many pagans became Christians at Antioch, and a man was soon to appear on the scene who would really bring the matter to a head. He was the greatest missionary of the early Church. His name was Saul, and his mission was specifically, although not exclusively, to the Gentiles.

He had been born of devout Jewish parents in Tarsus of Cilicia, and in this crossroads city he was subjected to all sorts of influences. Greek was his native, Aramaic his maternal, tongue. Staunch Jew though he was, he could not help learning a great deal about Greco-Roman culture; in fact, he had inherited the privilege of Roman citizenship from his father. But he was first and foremost a Jew, and when he went to Jerusalem for higher rabbinic studies, his knowledge of Judaism was deepened and his zeal inflamed to fever pitch.

Naturally he looked upon the Christian movement as an un-endurable apostasy, if not the worst of blasphemies, and had assisted at the stoning of Stephen with full approval. Not satis-fied with persecuting the Jerusalem Christians, he obtained authorization to go all the way up to Damascus to ferret out the renegades. But the road to Damascus turned out to be the road to Rome. When he was just a short distance from his goal he had a blinding vision of the risen Christ which trans-formed him on the spot from a persecutor to a promoter of the true religion. His natural zeal was now supernatural zeal, and his consuming hatred became a love which drove him to fantastic heights of heroism.

· Immediately after his baptism he began to preach the Good News in Damascus itself and in the outlying districts. This initial ministry lasted about three years. Then, after a visit to

Jerusalem, where he consulted with Peter, he returned to Tarsus. After he had been there for another three years or so, his good friend Barnabas came from the now flourishing church of Antioch and asked him to return thither with him. It was at Antioch that the followers of Christ were first called Christians. The name seems to have been invented by the pagans of the city as a contemptuous nickname for people whose lives were a standing reproach to their own.

Meanwhile the church in Jerusalem had fallen upon hard times, and an imminent famine threatened to aggravate their situation. Saul and Barnabas went down with a relief collection taken up at Antioch. Soon after their return to the Syrian capital, the church of that city held a departure ceremony which was to have far-reaching consequences. They sent Saul and Barnabas to Cyprus and then to the mainland on a missionary trip. Thus began what is known as the First Missionary Journey. After meeting with some success in Cyprus, Barnabas and Paul (from this point on he used his Gentile name) set sail for Asia Minor. They made a round-trip circuit of Perge, Antioch of Pisidia, Iconium, Lystra, and Derbe, all of which are in what is now south central Turkey.

Back in Antioch of Syria, the jubilant missionaries called together the brethren and told them of the powerful working of the grace of God among the Gentiles, and there was general rejoicing. But a group of reactionaries from the Jerusalem church insisted that circumcision was still necessary for salvation. This caused understandable consternation, and Paul, Barnabas, and a few others went down to Jerusalem to get the matter settled once for all. It was an extremely important matter; the future of the Church in the world depended on its correct solution.

Paul understood more clearly than anyone else in the early Church, with the possible exception of Peter, that the ritual observances of the Old Law were no longer necessary for salvation. He had no intention of imposing them on his Gentile converts, whom he loved and respected. At Jerusalem, Paul pleaded his cause before the apostles and the whole community. Peter backed him up wholeheartedly and cited the case of the Roman centurion, Cornelius. Even James, now bishop of Jerusalem and a loyal devotee of Jewish practices, admitted that obstacles should not be placed in the path of Gentiles wishing to enter the Kingdom. As a result of this meeting, the question was definitively settled, at least in principle. But, then as now, there were those who insisted on being "more Catholic than the Church," and they were to cause Paul and his converts no little trouble in the years that lay ahead.

The great missionary went on with his work, and in two more missionary journeys established churches throughout all of Asia Minor and Greece. He paid a high price for his success. He was heckled, beaten, stoned within an inch of his life, jailed, threatened with death — often. His health was none too robust, and traveling hundreds of miles in all kinds of weather — he went on foot most of the time — frequently brought on enervating illnesses. Only a heart heroically in love with Christ could have kept him going. But such was the heart of Paul, and it did not stop beating and loving until he was beheaded in Rome in 67 A.D.

Our picture of the birth and growth of the infant Church has been necessarily sketchy. We must now take a look at the inner life of that Church. What was it like to be a Christian in the first century? What did it mean? A Christian was first and foremost one who *believed,* and the object of his faith was the Lord Jesus Christ. One became a Christian, a believer, by listening to and accepting the Gospel message. This acceptance was not merely an intellectual assent to the truth or the beauty of the new doctrine, but a whole-souled embrace of all it implied, all it demanded.

Specifically, the faith which marked the Christian off from all other men consisted in an acknowledgment of Jesus as "the Lord." Flowing logically from this acknowledgment was an unswerving allegiance to His doctrine as announced and taught by His witnesses. The end result was a vital union with Him, a union which called for the unconditional surrender spoken of above. Thus the acceptance of the Christian message involved a conversion in the strictest sense of the term, a renunciation of the whole sin-filled past.

The Christian was not only a believer; he was also a "Baptized." Baptism was the external rite, the sacrament by which one became a member of the community of the faithful, for right from the beginning the Church was a well-defined, visible organization. It was not enough to believe; it was necessary also to belong, to be incorporated into the body of the Church, the Mystical Body of Christ, and one could gain entrance only by submitting to the sacred rite. It had a deep mystical significance which was clearly expressed in the manner in which it was commonly administered. The candidate was completely submerged beneath the water, "buried" with Christ, sharing the life-giving merits of His death on the Cross. The newly baptized rose from the water a new creature, sharing the sinless glory of the risen Savior. He had died to sin and self and had risen to a life intimately conjoined to that of the Lord in glory.

Associated with Baptism was the reception of the Holy Spirit. Usually this gift of the Spirit was separate from Baptism itself, and was often imparted by a distinct rite, the imposition of hands, as in Acts 8:17-18; 9:17; 19:6. Thus the new Christian was quite truly an "other Christ," for the Spirit of Christ Himself had come to fill his soul with His vivifying presence and action. Faith, Baptism, the indwelling of the Holy Spirit: these were the distinguishing characteristics of the Christian, who belonged no longer to himself, but to the Lord.

This union between Christ and His members was no pious fiction; it was a glorious reality, and they made it an ever more vital bond by praying to Him, often and fervently. In fact, prayer — individual and communal — was another distinguishing mark of the Christian. He believed, he was baptized, he loved, he *prayed*. The mother Church of Jerusalem, before the precise relationship of Christianity to Judaism became clear, lived close to the temple. And undoubtedly many elements of the temple — and synagogue — liturgy passed over into the Christian liturgy as the latter became a distinct form of worship. Right from the beginning, and more and more as time went on, the Christians met regularly by themselves. They had no churches, and so they held their services in the larger homes of the more well-to-do converts. Quite early they set aside the first day of the week as their special day of worship, and gradually it supplanted the Sabbath as "the Lord's day," the name given it in Apoc. 1:10.

The heart of the Christian service was the celebration of the Eucharist, know technically as the "breaking of the bread," as in Acts 2:42. This was the essential Christian rite, the sacrifice and sacrament which brought the individuals into mystical, yet very real, contact with the life-giving death and resurrection of the Savior, and into a union of love with each other.

"By this will all men know that you are my disciples, if you have love for one another" (John 13:35). The Book of Acts, in its little summaries of life in the early Church, has left us several sketches of the steps taken by the Christians to fulfill this wish of Jesus for them. "All the believers were united, and held all things in common. They would sell all their possessions and goods and distribute them as need required (2:44-45). Now the congregation of believers were of one heart and one soul. Not one of them claimed as his own anything he possessed. They held all things in common" (4:32).

We must not imagine, however, that all was sweetness and light among the first Christians. The selection of the first deacons was the result of a series of complaints that the Greek-speaking converts were being neglected in the distribution of funds from the common treasury. Not all of Paul's difficulties came from outside the Church by any means, and a reading of the first chapters of 1 Cor. will suffice to show that the human element was strong in the Church. Still, there was love and there was unity. Unity is not synonymous with uniformity, and the wonder of it all is that there should have been unity among so many people of so many backgrounds, temperaments, traditions, prejudices. Unity amid diversity is so much more striking than unity with uniformity. It evidences a principle of wondrous power, and that principle was ultimately the Holy Spirit and immediately the love of Christ beating in so many different hearts.

There was diversity, too, on the level of offices and functions, of which there was a surprising variety. As for offices, our Lord had taken care of the essential organization of the Church by selecting and commissioning "The Twelve" to teach and rule. Here, too, there was a strong center of unity: Peter, head of the Twelve. Then, too, assisting in the external and internal growth of the Church there were other ministries and functions. There were rulers, pastors, evangelists, prophets, teachers, servants, healers, etc. They were aided in a special way by the Holy Spirit, and their extraordinary capabilities were known as charisms or gifts. All contributed in various ways to the "building up of the Body of Christ," but though their gifts were diversified, they were all one: "But it is one and the same Spirit who is active in all these gifts, which he distributes just as he wishes. For example, just as the body is a unit, although it has many members, and all the members of the body, many though they are, form one body, so too is the Christ" (1 Cor. 12:11-12).

XX

THE RETURN OF CHRIST
AND THE ETERNAL KINGDOM

Salvation History reached its glorious climax in the passion, death, resurrection, and ascension of the Savior. It will continue to run its course until the end of time, until the Lord returns in final triumph to destroy completely, once for all, the power of Satan and to claim His kingdom for all eternity. The Second Coming, called technically the Parousia, was an integral element in our Lord's teaching and exerted a powerful influence on the thinking of the apostolic Church. In fact, the early Christians were quite taken up with the thought of Jesus' return in glory, and some of them entertained some rather strange notions on the subject. St. Paul had to write two letters to the Thessalonians to correct such notions.

Their confusion is understandable, however. Our Lord revealed this doctrine only very gradually and, for reasons prompted by His divine wisdom and prudence, not too clearly as far as details of time and manner were concerned. Hence many of His individual remarks were open to misunderstanding. It was only in retrospect and with the new understanding which their Pentecostal faith brought them that the apostles arrived at a balanced appreciation of the doctrine. They, too, had looked for a definitive establishment of the messianic kingdom during the lifetime of Jesus. Recall their disputes about precedence in the Kingdom and the request of James and John that they be allowed to occupy places at the right and left of Jesus' throne. Had He not proclaimed, among other things, that "the kingdom of heaven is at hand"?

Their hopes, dampened by predictions of the Passion and dashed by the Crucifixion, revived after the Resurrection. On the way to the Mount of Ascension they asked Him expectantly, "Lord, wilt thou at this time restore the kingdom to Israel?" But he said to them, "It is not for you to know the times or dates which the Father has fixed by his own authority; but you shall receive power when the Holy Spirit comes upon you, and you shall be witnesses for me in Jerusalem and in all Judea and Samaria and even to the very ends of the earth" (Acts 1:6-8).

Little by little, then, they came to understand that the really definitive establishment of the Kingdom in all its perfection would come only after an indefinite period of relatively imperfect existence here on earth. The care which Jesus had taken to organize a Church with a view to its functioning in the world was an indication of what the situation actually was to be. They knew that Jesus would come again in glory. After the Ascension the angel had assured them: "This Jesus who has been taken up from you into heaven, will come in the same way as you have seen him going up to heaven" (Acts 1:11). Of this they were sure. The uncertain element was the exact time of His return. He had absolutely refused to give them even a hint on this score. They had only His scattered references to ponder, and they were none too clear, at least for the general body of the faithful.

The longest single statement of our Lord's on the subject of His second coming was the so-called Eschatological Discourse in Matt. 24 and the parallel passages in Mark and Luke. This discourse is difficult to explain; it seems to fluctuate between the destruction of Jerusalem and the end of the world. Recently, however, a very convincing exegesis has been proposed which sees the whole discourse as a prophecy of the destruction of Jerusalem. The style is quite clearly that of the Old Testament prophecies, particularly those of the apocalyptic type, which employed flamboyant symbolism and described historical occurrences in terms of cosmic disasters. Interpreting the discourse in the light of this style, one can without difficulty refer to the fall of Jerusalem those verses which at first sight seem to point to an event of far greater proportions. In this interpretation, then, Jesus would be describing in apocalyptic language His triumphant return in judgment on the city which had rejected Him. This return within the framework of history would in turn be a type or figure of His final glorious Parousia at the end of time.

The discourse was occasioned by a question of the disciples. They had been admiring the temple buildings when our Lord remarked, "Do you see all these things? Amen I say to you, there will not be left here one stone upon another that will not be thrown down." Later, the disciples asked Him, "Tell us, when are these things to happen, and what will be the sign of thy coming and of the end of the world?" (Matt. 24:1-3). The first part of their question clearly refers to the destruction of the temple. For them that marked the end of the Jewish world; they could not imagine Judaism without the temple. It would be the end of the old era and the beginning of the new. With this change they associated Jesus' coming, His glorious manifestation; it would mark "the end of the world," that is, the end of the Jewish world. As a matter of fact, the Greek word used by Matthew for "world" here signifies era, epoch. Thus their question would really bear on the one event, the destruction of Jerusalem, and so would Jesus' answer. Significantly, their question in Luke is simply, "Master, when are these things to happen, and what will be the sign when these things will begin to come to pass?" (Luke 21:7).

It is impossible to study this long passage in detail; suffice it to say that the explanation just outlined has a great deal to recommend it. If it is the correct one, it throws much light on some other difficult passages in the gospel. To mention just one: when Jesus sent His disciples on their trial preaching mission, He warned them of the hardships and persecutions which would attend their missionary work and advised them, when persecution broke out in one town, to flee to another. Then He remarked: "Amen I say to you, you will not have gone through the towns of Israel before the Son of Man comes" (Matt. 10:23). If one takes His "coming" as the final one at the end of the world His words are quite difficult to explain. If, however, one understands it of His coming in judgment on Jerusalem, the difficulty vanishes. For the city fell to the Romans in 70 A.D., and not all of Palestine had been evangelized by then.

Whatever be the literal interpretation of the Eschatological Discourse, it refers at least typically to Jesus' coming in glory to judge the world at the end of time. His judgment of Jerusalem was to serve as a preview of His universal judgment. And His constantly repeated warning was "Watch!" This warning He intended for all men of all time: "Take heed, watch and pray, for you do not know when the time is: just as a man, when he leaves home to journey abroad, puts his servants in charge, to each his work, and gives orders to the porter to keep watch. Watch, therefore, for you do not know when the master of the house is coming, in the evening, or at midnight, or at cockcrow, or early in the morning; lest coming suddenly he find you sleeping. *And what I say to you, I say to all, 'Watch'"* (Mark 13: 33-37). "Watch therefore, for you do not know at what hour your Lord is to come. But of this be assured, that if the householder had known at what hour the thief was coming, he certainly would have watched, and not have let his house be broken into. Therefore you must also be ready, because at an hour that you do not expect, the Son of Man will come" (Matt. 24: 42-44). The parables of the Ten Virgins and of the Talents issue the same serious admonition (Matt. 25:1-30).

Jesus left us a picturesquely beautiful portrayal of the Last Judgment; it is recorded in Matt. 25:31-46. "But when the Son of Man shall come in his majesty, and all the angels with him, then he will sit on the throne of his glory; and before him will be gathered all the nations, and he will separate them one from another, as the shepherd separates the sheep from the goats; and he will set the sheep on his right hand, but the goats on his left." Jesus then describes the meting out of reward or punishment; the determining factor will be the exercise or neglect of the great Christian virtue of charity, that love which is the fulfillment of the Law.

Our Lord's teaching on the Second Coming formed an important part of the preaching of the early Church. St. Paul's epistles are full of explicit and offhand allusions to "the coming of the Lord." The reality of this event deeply colored the thinking of the first Christians. Recent studies on the meaning of the Our Father in the early Church have shown that the Christian community of the first century, anxiously expecting the second coming, prayed that God would completely glorify His name by establishing His kingdom, which represented the fulfillment of the plan He had willed for both earth and heaven. The community also asked for a place at the heavenly banquet table to break bread with the Christ, and a forgiveness of its sins. A titanic struggle with Satan stood between the community and the realization of its prayer and from this trial it asked to be delivered. The Eucharist, too, had eschatological overtones. It was a foretaste of the messianic banquet to be enjoyed in the eternal Kingdom. It is interesting to recall in this connection how frequently Jesus linked the Eucharist with blessed immortality in the discourse in John 6. To cite but one example: "This is the bread that comes down from heaven, so that if anyone eat of it he will not die. I am the living bread that has come down from heaven. If anyone eat of this bread he shall live forever; and the bread that I will give is my flesh for the life of the world" (John 6:50-52).

It is not too surprising that misunderstanding arose among the faithful on the question of the Parousia. But that misunderstanding had the happy result of prompting St. Paul to give an authentic statement on the matter. The Thessalonians' first difficulty, answered in Paul's first letter to them, had to do with the fate of those who had already died. What part would they play in the glorious return of the Lord? Paul assured them that when He came, their beloved dead would be at no disadvantage. They would first rise from the dead and then, together with the living, would take part in the triumphant procession to the Kingdom. He also reminded them of the uncertainty of the time of the Parousia.

This reminder did not bear full fruit. Several of the Christians of Thessalonica, convinced that the great day was just around the corner, had quit working, saw no point in marrying and establishing a home, and thus created a most unrealistic and unhealthy situation. In his second letter, then, Paul had to be quite clear on the time of the Second Coming. "We beseech you . . . not to be hastily shaken from your right mind, nor terrified . . . as though the day of the Lord were near at hand" (2 Thess. 2:1-2). He then went on to list all the events which were to take place before Christ would come again. His description of those events is cryptic, to say the least; he had already explained them to the Thessalonians and felt it sufficient merely to allude to them in his letter. But he does touch on a theme which turns up elsewhere, especially in St. John's Apocalypse: before the end of the world comes, Satan will make one more desperate, all-out, effort to snatch mankind from the loving hands of God. And he will meet with some success; there will be a great apostasy and the forces of evil will have a heyday. But in a final struggle of cosmic proportions, Jesus will triumph completely and definitively and establish His eternal kingdom in which good will reign unopposed.

The teaching of the Apostle on the essentials of the matter is quite clear. The Lord will definitely come again in brilliant triumph, but the time of that coming is most uncertain. It could take place soon, but the indications are that a considerable span of time will intervene. This seems to have been the general attitude of the first Christians. They looked forward hopefully to the definitive establishment of the Kingdom and, indeed, prayed that is might take place soon: "Thy kingdom come!" "And the Spirit and the bride (the Church) say, 'Come!' And let him who hears say, 'Come!' Amen! Come, Lord Jesus!" (Apoc. 22:17, 20).

The characteristic Christian attitude is one of expectation, of waiting, of hope. In the words of St. Paul to the Hebrews (13: 14), "We have not here a lasting city." For each of us, the Second Coming may take place at any moment, and that coming is really all that gives meaning to our lives. "Behold, I stand at the door and knock. If any man listens to my voice and opens the door to me, I will come in to him and sup with him, and he with me. He who overcomes, I will permit him to sit with me upon my throne; as I also have overcome and have sat with my Father on his throne" (Apoc. 3:20-21). "And what I say to you, I say to all, 'Watch' " (Mark 13:37).

But over and above this individual coming to each Christian there will be the great and glorious Parousia at the end of time. This is the event which will inaugurate the final phase, the eternal phase of Salvation History. It is the one event which gives full meaning to that history and, indeed, to all of human history. Apart from it man's sojourn on earth is a cruel farce, an illusory groping in the dark for an unknown object, a maddening swing from optimism to pessimism and back again, a dead-end street at the end of which lurks crushing despair. But in its light, life is richly meaningful, purposeful, worth while. For it casts over all of life's vicissitudes the cheering aura of God's infinite love, that love which started Salvation History on its course and will bring it to its brilliant conclusion.

"These are they who have come out of the great tribulation, and have washed their robes and made them white in the blood of the Lamb. Therefore they are before the throne of God, and serve him day and night in his temple, and he who sits upon the throne will dwell with them. They shall neither hunger nor thirst any more, neither shall the sun strike them nor any heat. For the Lamb who is in the midst of the throne will shepherd them, and will guide them to the fountains of the waters of life, and God will wipe away every tear from their eyes" (Apoc. 7:14-17).

> "Eye has not seen nor ear heard,
> Nor has it entered into the heart of man,
> What things God has prepared for those who love him"
> (1 Cor. 2:9).